THE ROOT OF THE MATTER

The Root of the Matter

Essays by

J. D. Beresford   Lionel Birch

J. S. Collis   H. W. Heckstall-Smith

H. R. L. Sheppard

Edited by

H. R. L. SHEPPARD

with a Foreword

Essay Index Reprint Series

BOOKS FOR LIBRARIES PRESS, INC.

FREEPORT, NEW YORK

First published 1937
Reprinted 1967

LIBRARY OF CONGRESS CATALOG NUMBER:

67-26784

PRINTED IN THE UNITED STATES OF AMERICA

FOREWORD

NEARLY all of us feel that there is something wrong with the general conditions of modern life, and nearly all, too, cast about for a way of putting things right, though for the most part we come to differing conclusions as to what is wrong, and follow differing theories as to how things should be righted. That we should make any effort towards amelioration is good, but that we should make such differing and opposite efforts tends towards cancellation: while we remain a house divided, we shall, to say the least, get little done.

This book, while it tries to avoid being dogmatic or didactic, is the attempt of five independent writers on different subjects to reach the root of the matter where what is wrong is concerned. But it is a further attempt than that, for the five writers, when the root of the matter has been exposed by a certain amount of apparently destructive spade-work, have tried to build up, still independently within their own subjects, a constructive proposal for a better state of affairs.

The five subjects were chosen because they seemed to be of paramount importance; to be, in another sense, the root of the matter of ordinary daily life. They are subjects, surely, in which every man and woman must take an interest.

Only on the surface, however, are they really independent of one another, and only on the surface, though they wrote without consulting one another, are the writers independent. Since all five live in a particular period of the world's restless history, since they must have been subjected to similar experiences, have reacted and suffered similarly and been filled with similar hopes of delivery and progress, it is not unnatural that the inferences they draw from the conditions obtaining in their several subjects, the conclusions they reach and the proposals they offer, should also in the end show themselves similar. And in the same way, the five subjects, like those who write on them, if only because they are parts of a common subject known as everyday life, inevitably interlock, their matter overlaps, their writers encroach upon one another's territory. So we hope that this book of seeming independencies finally unites into something of a whole, comes to a common conclusion and escapes cancelling itself out by coming to opposite conclusions. We do not presume to offer anything so pretentious as a universal remedy. The universal remedy, if he believes that there is one, is for the reader to infer. But we do hope that we have at least to some extent achieved a common purpose: that of helping, if only a little, those interested in these subjects, to a greater understanding of the problems that we all face, and to the discovery of the root of the matter, whence the next step is that of transplanting the tree of life in a soil where it will be the better able to flourish.

H.R.L.S.

CONTENTS

I
HUMAN RELATIONS
J. D. BERESFORD

HUMAN RELATIONS

I

IF we could truly get to the root of the matter in this problem of human relationships, root and flower and all, we should know what God and Man is.

We can write of politics, the money-market, engineering, literature, science, the arts, and a host of other fascinating subjects without any need to go beyond the limits of that intellectually realizable, phenomenal world whose infinite variety is the source of all our knowledge. We are dealing with products, and any inquiry as to origins is irrelevant to the discussion. The original mystery, as such, must be taken for granted. Everything comes from the egg, and we are talking not of eggs, but of what is hatched from them. Your botanist plucks the flower from the crannied wall, and picks it to pieces, classifies it as belonging to this or that family, or if he is in luck, as a rare hybrid; and he is perfectly right in doing no more than that. He is a botanist, not a poet, nor a mystic, and his knowledge may be of great use to the world. He may, for instance, be able to teach us how to breed and produce a disease-resisting wheat and so reduce the price of flour. That is the way of knowledge, hardly

3

won through the exercise of observation and reason, the way of all the Sciences, exact or inexact, the way of mankind pursuing his little adventure between birth and death, and passing on some fragment of the knowledge he has gained from generation to generation.

And there is, of course, a possibility of treating human relationships by this method. Instead of attempting any answer to the vast question "What is Man?" we can regard him as a phenomenon of this three-dimensional, temporal world. We can, indeed, very easily lose ourselves in this aspect of our problem, which will open up the discussion of such engrossing topics as sociology, justice, ethics, education and, inevitably, psychology,—all of them appropriate to our thesis and rich with opportunities for argument, suggestions and dogma. But, although we may and, indeed, must begin by this method we cannot end with it, unless we are content to declare ourselves from the outset as convinced materialists. If I could do that, I might write a rational and possibly instructive essay, but it would have no root.

If man is no more than the ephemeral product of an unknown and unknowable life force, then all talk of human relationships becomes an academic question, and would not, in my opinion, be worth discussing. Nevertheless it will be necessary, as has been said, to treat man in the first place as a product—whether of an evolutionary system or of an act of special creation, makes no difference for the time being—to regard him as a phenomenon, temporarily separated from any past or future we may postulate for him, passing from birth to old age.

To do this with any effectiveness a preliminary simplification is advisable, and I propose to find it in the myth of Adam and Eve. All the myths that survive are rich in psychological parables and as Bernard Shaw has said in "Back to Methuselah" that "The most scientific document we possess at present is . . . the story of the Garden of Eden," it should afford us trustworthy material.

No greater simplification of human relations is possible than this opposition of the only living man and woman on earth, set down in idyllic surroundings and yet making a terrible mess of it. But a reason for their failure to live happily in their earthly paradise can be inferred with little trouble. It must have been a difference of temperament.

Adam was content to obey the one simple law of restraint that had been laid upon him. He had his companion, his animals and his garden, and found in them a sufficient occupation. He had no thought of past or future to trouble him since all the days he remembered were of the same pattern, and so far as he could see, would continue to be of the same pattern throughout eternity. He had never known any other life, and was unable to imagine one.

Eve was similarly circumstanced, and we must assume that she accepted her condition in the same spirit as Adam, but she had a quality that he lacked. The serpent in her garden was that vice which we have since been compelled to elevate into a virtue, the vice

5

of curiosity. It was not the scientific curiosity that will compel a man to a single line of research throughout his adult life, but the primitive curiosity of the wild animal. She did not want to know for any particular purpose, she was just inquisitive, with the simple inquisitiveness of a child. She thought, no doubt, that it would be nice to see what would happen if she did the only thing that she had been told not to do.

The outstanding reason, then, for the failure of Adam and Eve to make a success of their life in the garden, was this difference of temperament. His was the type of peace-loving man, content to stay in his rut, to do the same things every day in the same way, and he hated to be bothered. He probably ate his share of the apple to avoid bother with Eve, whose voice was so much nearer and more threatening than that other Voice belonging to the remote presence who walked in the garden at even. Adam had the makings of a good Fascist. He liked to be regimented. It saved trouble.

Eve, afflicted by her inquisitive temperament, could not leave anything alone. I have no doubt that long before that unfortunate business with the apple, she had been in the habit of stirring Adam up a bit, just to see what he would do. I can picture her asking him to come for a walk when he was settling down for his afternoon's nap, and taking him away from his animals because she wanted to talk to him for a bit. "To talk? But good Garden of Eden what about?", Adam probably said, and Eve "Oh nothing

6

particular, just talk. Surely you've been messing about long enough with those old lions of yours?". Even if there had been no forbidden tree, there would have been a split sooner or later, although they might have gone on living together for the sake of the children. Theirs was one of those relationships that do not make for happiness. Speaking from the platform of the detached, scientific lecturer, we may label our instance as one of incompatible temperament, a pregnant cause in the modern world of battle, murder and sudden death. The Latins and the Teutons suffer from this trouble.

In the seclusion of our fabulous Eden, with only two human beings to consider we have separated a single cause for disharmony, but now the problem must be complicated by innumerable other factors introduced by the multiplication of numbers and the needs of civilization. We have to consider from our scientific platform, something at least of how this question of human relations is affected in dealing with gregarious man, living in vast cities, men of all grades of intelligence and physical ability, compelled to come into contact with one another, work and play together, whether their temperaments, tastes and what we call characters are compatible or not. Economic necessity, not less than our gregarious habit, enforce these contacts, and as sociologists and psychologists, with that strong ethical bias which must be postulated as a part of our outfit, we have to contemplate some plan for the establishment of a condition in which men can live together in harmony.

2

We must retain our primitive element. Incompatibility of temperament will do well enough to represent the great diversity of taste, tendency, character that separates one man from the next, and mav vary so widely that they become unintelligible to each other. Imagine for example the difficulty of communication between an elderly University Don who has devoted the best part of his life to the study of Greek, and an agricultural labourer of the same age, who has read nothing since he left the National School at fourteen and never been farther then ten miles from his native village.

Picture them shut up together by some accident for six hours with nothing to do but talk to each other. It is perhaps rather a significant comment on such a terrible situation, that I can imagine the Don learning something from the labourer in the course of that conversation, but not the remotest possibility of the labourer learning anything from the Don. As the negro mother said to her son, "if you've no education you've just got to use your brains."

This may be rather an extreme instance of the incompatibility we shall have to deal with in planning our Utopia, but we must recognize not only that such extremes exist but that they provide an illustration of certain types produced by modern civilization. And I would point out further, that the gulf between Don and labourer is not one that could be bridged by a drastic revision of our methods of education. If those two had been at school together and met again after fifty years they would still have lacked any such mutual interest, as might have provided them with a means of communication. Two old boys from the same public school, who had lived very different lives would find very little to say to one another if they met again at the age of sixty. After they had got through the preliminary interchanges that are paragraphed by the opening questions, "Do you remember so and so. Do you know what became of him?" they would probably fall into silence, especially if they differed widely in their political and religious views.

Nevertheless this problem of education, even if it is not ultimately a fundamental cause of the separation of men from their fellows, is one that has an enormous influence on human relations in ordinary life. It is not fundamental because all men are not equally educable, but the provision of a means to give every child the same opportunities in this matter of learning, must be one of the chief planks in the platform of the Utopist who desires to inaugurate the Age of Harmony. "Give me control of a child up to the age of seven and you can do what you like with him afterwards," said the Jesuit father, and for a moment we may play with the idea of a World State in which all the teachers were in agreement as to precisely what the child should be taught up to the age of seven.

But the possibility is so infinitely remote that it would be a waste of time to consider it. And what, one wonders, would be the result. A hive? Or an ant-hill? The Utopia that has for its object the elimination of diversity is condemned from the outset. It could only be retrogressive.

9

But having granted the necessity for a drastic revision of our educational policy leaving the resultant practice for discussion by a companion essayist, we have to go a step farther back and consider the main obstacle to be overcome before any such revision of present economic conditions is possible. And no discussion of human relations can be made, from our present platform, without a serious inquiry into what is surely one of the most important factors in the dissension between man and man.

At this point, however, the lecturer lays down his chalk, temporarily abandons his notes, and makes a personal explanation to his audience. "I must ask you," he says, "to regard me in what I have now to say, as nothing more than an impersonal mind. I am not going to speak to you as a Communist, Marxist, Collectivist, Socialist, Liberal, Conservative, as in short the representative of any shade of political opinion.

It is true that we are in a sense planning some kind of Utopia, but the details of construction must be left to the builders. My subject is "Human Relations," and I am trying to treat it without prejudice on an Ethico-Sociological basis, assuming the human race as an aggregate of diverse units which for practical reasons we have to classify under comparatively few headings. At the beginning of the next section, you will, quite inevitably, I think, be inclined to regard me as a thorough-going political Socialist. But if you will bear with me until I have finished, you will realize that I have only been stating a case from which you are at liberty to draw any conclusion that may accord with your own political creed. We will now resume our definitions."

It cannot be denied, in the first place, that the perpetual observation of the contrast between wealth so great that the immense superfluity is useless to its possessor, and the physical miseries of extreme poverty, is little likely to conduce to harmonious relations between rich and poor. History shows that when the contrast becomes too great it so far effects the sympathies of the middle class intelligentsia that they urge the masses to revolt. The result when such a revolution has been directed against the land-owning class has so far done little more than substitute a comparatively intelligent plutocracy for the comparatively unintelligent autocracy that preceded it, a development that is still possible in Bolshevik Russia. An impassioned revolution can never in fact, do anything to ameliorate human relations. Its first effect is to reverse the positions of the upper and under-dogs, its second to revert to the old conditions under a different denomination.

In Great Britain, the recognition that revolution provides no remedy for poverty has kept our more earnest reformers in check. Our Northern blood may simmer now and again, but it does not boil over. We are a temperate people. Our reformers advocate the principles of an evolutionary socialism and our most fervent reactionaries make occasional concessions to our immediate needs. Even our newspaper proprietors maintain their circulations on the assumption that the public may be led but cannot be driven. And in no

11

other country has the acceptance of humaneness as a necessary factor of civilization been more influential than it has in England, even if our humaneness be more noticeable in our treatment of animals than in our treatment of humanity.

In England, then, if anywhere, we should find the promise of a future Age of Harmony, in which, although we can never eliminate that fundamental incompatability of temperament we found in the Garden of Eden, men would be able to work together without quarrelling. Let us inquire, therefore, how these economic conditions we are examining, serve to retard our progress.

Well, speaking, as I would remind you in the person of the ethically-minded sociologist, I must begin with the unqualified admission that the greatest bar to decent human relations is imposed by the patent and exceedingly well-advertised contrast between the lives of the rich and the poor. It is, and can never conceivably fail to be, a perpetual cause of envy, hatred, malice and all uncharitableness. The multitude of the poor must always envy the rich, and the rich fear the poor, because they are so many. Nor is the effect of this dissension-making contrast confined to the two extremes. That sympathetic intelligentsia, referred to as the stimulators of revolution, the class from which so many of our active political socialists are recruited, react violently against the rule of wealth and become the haters of those that impose their will upon the people. Thus, the class-war though it may not be fought with poison-gas and machine-guns, is continually in being—"class" having become, now, almost exclusively a question of income. For hate must always find its ultimate expression in fighting. Hate means the desire to kill, a desire that is restrained only by consideration for the killer's own safety. And so long as there is a class with far too much money and a class with far too little, one cannot hope for decent human relations between them.

There are of course, a very large number of exceptions to this rule as between individuals representing the opposed classes. Not every millionaire is a villain to his valet, nor even an object of envy. There are also, apparent exceptions in the relations that may be established between employers and employed. Indeed, in the latter connexion, there has been for half-a-century a steadily increasing realization by employers of labour that their best hope of avoiding trouble is to keep labour contented by making its workshops and its homes as hygienic and comfortable as possible. In certain famous experiments, whose example is being followed by other enterprises of the same kind, the care for the workpeople has been extended to providing them with entertainment for their leisure, theatres, libraries, and the means to develop any hobby they may fancy. But such exceptions as these do very little to mitigate the essential trouble. So long as the few have too much money and there are millions on or near the poverty-line, we can never hope to enter that Age of Harmony which has been posed as our ideal.

This conclusion I believe to be indisputable, but it

does not follow that the only remedy is some form of political socialism. If this nation were allowed to live in peace with its neighbours, if during a period of national prosperity the workers were sufficiently well-paid and well-housed to live in comfort, if under a wise and paternal Government no man or woman who was employable could be out of work, and that floating population of a quarter of a million or so of unemployables was provided for, if, in short, abject poverty were impossible and the general standard of living were raised, should we not get rid of that resentment and rancour in the poorer classes that continually militates against the establishment of human relations between the rulers and the ruled? The Communist replies with an emphatic "No," insisting that no man can face his fellow men on equal terms so long as he remains a wage-slave. The Conservatives and the Church, though not perhaps for quite the same reasons, reply with a not less emphatic "Yes." I leave the issue open to be decided between them, with the reminder that the contingents postulated, peace, national prosperity and wise Government are ideals that have yet to be realized —a consummation that will be attained with great difficulty if it is to be sought by opposing political parties with incompatible views on the ends to be attained, and the means to obtain them.

Our sociological argument has taken us back step by step to the consideration of increasing backgrounds. Beginning with a single pair, we dealt next with education, and then with the economic difficulties that lie behind that problem. Now we have to forsake the concept of a single people and try, on the basis we have already established, to think of the world as a whole.

It will be as well to begin by the bald statement that at the present time anything like a decent human relation between one nation and another is almost impossible. There may be *ententes*, pacts and written agreements of many kinds, but they are based on mutual political interests, not on the understanding of one nation for another, and certainly not on affection, —to use the mildest of our verbal substitutes for love. A remedy is being sought by the few for this unhappy condition. In the course of the past fifteen years or so, we have heard much talk of internationalism and seen a few tentative efforts made to encourage a common understanding between European nations, by such experiments as exchange parties of young student visitors. There have been plans for the establishment of international schools. Also for much longer than fifteen years certain writers, most prominently H. G. Wells, have demonstrated on paper beyond all possibility of contradiction that the only hope of an enduring peace lies in a true internationalism, a brotherhood of man united by a common understanding and a common aim. And we have the League of Nations.

There, in effect, is our plan. Could any plan be more admirable? But what is the present position, what the hope, if any, of furthering our ambition in the course of the next generation? To answer these questions, we shall do well to take a brief glance at the conditions obtaining in the larger States of Europe.

15

In Germany, between whom and ourselves there are
ties of blood and temperament which should make for
affection and understanding, we are confronted primarily by the tremendous obstacle of a dictatorship.
Now a dictatorship never represents the will of the
whole people although it may carry on for years supported on the shoulders of a comparatively small but
powerful minority. Moreover, a dictatorship suffers in
a violently aggravated form from the evil present in our
own political system, the need for remaining in power.
The dictator if he is to remain a dictator has to be an
opportunist. He must take advantage of the weakness
of the people he governs because the weaknesses are
more ductible than the virtues, and so much more in
evidence. Adolf Hitler has been able to retain power
over Germany almost entirely by waving the flag of
nationalism. It is the largest common factor upon
which he can work, and he has worked it to a pitch at
which it has become ridiculous from the ethnologist's
point of view. He has been exceptionally favoured by
the fact that the German nation has been suffering for
eighteen years under the oppressions and disabilities
heaped upon her by the treaty of Versailles. His
attitude towards Europe has been of the same nature as
the attitude of the underpaid employee to the rich
owner of our earlier instance, resentful, grudging, with
an increasing undercurrent of angry self-assertion. And
so long as Germany remains content to be guided by
Hitler—her only hope at the present time—internationalism between her and ourselves is quite impossible. We may arrive at an understanding with her,

but it will be founded on mutual political aims not on any consideration for the brotherhood of man nor for the common good of Europe. For the present we cannot hope to do much in the furtherance of human relations with Germany.

The case of Italy, although there, too, we are faced with the same difficulty of a dictator-led people, is of a different kind. There is not here the same social sympathy as there is between ourselves and Germany, but there is a tradition of friendship and common purpose that dates back to the middle of the last century. Moreover, despite that fundamental incompatibility of temperament between the Latin and Teutonic races, English and Italians, condoning each other's weaknesses, can live together in unity more successfully than the English and the French; possibly because the Italians are farther apart from us than the French, both in blood and mileage. Nevertheless this vague feeling of friendship is a very flimsy thing. It was all but blown to rags in the Autumn of 1935, and one further step on the part of England at that time, such as the attempt to close the Suez Canal, would have led to her name being reviled and spat upon from Tuscany to Sicily. Even as things are there can be little left of the good-feeling that has become a sort of tradition since the days of the Risorgimento, far too little for us to count upon her as an ally unless our interests ran together. All of which goes to prove, for our present purpose, that we are still a very long way from the hope of establishing a satisfactory human relation with the Italian people, even if their destinies and their inclinations

17

were not swayed by a Dictator whose policy is influenced ultimately by the desire to retain his own office.

As to France, I have already said that the average Englishman is less likely to make friends with a Frenchman than with an Italian. France is our nearest neighbour in Europe and the tradition of social rivalries and hatreds that have endured for more than eight centuries is not easily lived down. The dislike of England is much more noticeable in the North, (especially Normandy), than in the South; and my personal experience goes to show that the innate mistrust of England does not exist in the partly Italianized Provence. For, indeed, there is more difference between the Norman and the Provençal than between the Scotsman and the Englishman. The truth is that the French and the English are just near enough and, in some respects, alike enough, to get on each other's nerves. They are annoyed by our complacent self-sufficiency and what they regard as our hypocrisy. We distrust their lack of sentiment, and of humaneness which are, to us, the most noticeable aspects of their logicality. Even when they were fighting together against a common enemy the Tommy and the Poilu could not fraternize. Nevertheless, although there are immense difficulties to be overcome, it is surely not impossible that in the course of a generation or two a genuine unity might exist between the English and the French. There must be, as in all friendships, a certain amount of give and take. When the Englishman has acquired the smatterings of cosmopolitanism, and ceased to regard his more nimble-witted neighbour as the representative of an inferior race, and the Frenchman on his side has learnt that much of what appeared to him as "perfidy" was due to our queer puritanical national conscience, we ought to be able to hit it off together reasonably well.

It would be absurd to attempt any forecast with regard to our future relations with Russia or of Russia's relations with the rest of Europe. In the last few years there has been a recognizable reaction against Leninism, a tendency to return not to Capitalism but to a far milder form of socialism than that advocated by the ardent followers of Karl Marx at the beginning of the century. Should Russia be compelled to open the doors of her vast concentration camp and allow the influence of free opinion to reach that generation whose training has so far been as dogmatic as that prescribed by the Jesuit of the earlier instance, a still greater reaction will be inevitable among her young people. Meanwhile we know that the ideals of the U.S.S.R. are absolutely opposed to those of Germany and Italy, and are not regarded sympathetically by a majority of the electorate in France and England. For which reason any chance of establishing friendly relations with Russia are at present very remote.

This exceedingly brief summary of the present situation in Europe, so far as it relates to our immediate subject, affords small prospect of taking even the first steps towards such an understanding between the nations as would lead to that far hope, the Parliament of Man, the Federation of the World. We have been encouraged by the belief that the enormously increased facilities of intercommunication between one country and another made possible by the astonishing advances in invention, during the twentieth century, would serve to break down the bristling defences of nationalism. We are constantly reminded that we no longer live on an island protected by the sea from foreign invasion, and that the use of air-ways and the influence of broadcasting will serve to destroy national barriers. But there are few indications of that hope at the present moment. Europe's rulers are reverting, whether or not against their inclinations, to the old discredited principle of the balance of power and the making of defensive (we now carefully omit in any public statement the implicit "and offensive") alliances, the one really effective instrument they can use to win national approval being the inflammation of a hysterical patriotism. The effect of this policy leads straight to War. No other arbitrament is possible. And yet we are constantly being told, and are perfectly willing to believe, that another large-scale war will be the end of civilization for fifty years. Most shades of well-informed opinion seem to be agreed as to that, wherefore we must conclude that the rulers of Europe are doing all they can to bring about the conditions that will ultimately destroy us. But the destruction of civilization means nothing to a Stalin, a Hitler or a Mussolini. They hope to win, and to survive. And as only a war of extermination would really serve their purpose, we might as well boldly adopt the slogan

"Exterminate or be exterminated." Now that we frankly subscribe to the belief that in the next war, no one will be immune, civilians, cripples, the aged, women and children, we may just as well be honest and discuss the possibility of destroying a whole nation as we would drown a superfluous kitten. In war any attempt to establish human relations between ourselves and those who are, technically our enemies, is regarded as a traitor.

All this is as depressing as the reading of the foreign news in our morning paper; but we may end our survey on a faint note of optimism. For if the four great nations cited are at present unapproachable, Scandinavia is not. Norway, Sweden and Denmark have much in common with ourselves, and Holland may very well be added to the list. None of them is hysterically nationalistic, that is to say they are not passionately eager to impose their own opinions with regard to race, culture or what not on their neighbours; and they have no desire to wage a war of aggression either for this purpose or to facilitate colonial expansion. We are on good terms with those four countries and might with advantage cultivate their closer friendship, not with any idea of forming a military alliance, but simply in order that we might come to know one another very much better than we do. A true friendship between nations, as between individuals, must be based on liking, not on any consideration of mutual advantage. The latter may be necessary for a business partnership, but the moment self-seeking enters as an important factor in friendship, love flies out of the window. And if "love" between two nations may seem a very distant ideal, it should at least, be the goal of our ultimate ambition.

We would suggest, then, that by way of laying the first foundation of a true internationalism, we might very well make some kind of beginning by trying to understand the character and sympathize with the ideals of Norway, Denmark, Sweden, and Holland. There are no insuperable obstacles in the way. They are our own kind in many ways, and since none of them is predominantly a military nation, our overtures would not unduly excite the suspicions and jealousies of the remainder of Europe. The suggestion of encouraging the existing good-feeling between them and us, has not, and is not designed to have, any political advantage or significance, but it would be an admirable exercise in the undoubtedly very difficult art of loving one's neighbours as oneself. That advice to-day, as we know by the experience of nineteen hundred years, is a counsel of perfection, and we must not look for immediate results. But surely it is worth trying. And even if we have so far ignominiously failed to love our next door neighbour, a little practice with our neighbour overseas could not conceivably do us any harm.

In conclusion, says our ethico-sociological lecturer, let us briefly summarize the very extensive ground over which we have travelled. We began with a single pair of human beings in idyllic surroundings and found them coming to odds, by reason of incompatibility of temperament. That factor has not been eliminated by our subsequent inquiries into the state of man, but our implication throughout has been that this fundamental diversity of character between one man and the next has been encouraged and exaggerated by the pressure and exigencies of civilization. We brought forward three main instances of this in (1) education, (2) social conditions and (3) international relations.

In the first instance we pointed out to what extent men are separated from one another by early training, even to such extremes that, as in the case of the Don and the Agricultural Labourer, two Compatriots may have no means of intercourse. Our remedy for this difficulty was obvious, namely that every child should have the same opportunities for learning in its youth, a remedy that is at present impossible because it necessitates a revision in vital particulars of our second instance—social conditions.

In considering this we found a powerful enlargement of our main theme by a brief examination of the effects of dissension produced by the extremes of riches and poverty. It was shown, and the conclusion is undeniable, that these extremes are a factor still more potent even than education, in the separation of man from his fellows, that evil has divided man into two separate classes, each hating and fearing the other, with an intermediate class, in which we find the more intelligent and more ethically-minded members siding with the poor and seeking a remedy either by revolution or by social reform.

The particular political means by which that remedy can be obtained did not fall within the scope of our

23   3

lecture, but it is becoming every day more obvious that unless some remedy is found by peaceful measures, it will inevitably be found in war. At the moment of writing, September 1936, Spain is in the throes of a terrible civil war in order to decide whether a communist or a fascist government is to rule the people. But whatever the outcome, it is certain that victor and vanquished will be no nearer to living in amity one with the other. War never has, and never can, decide anything to the satisfaction of both parties.

In the analysis of our third instance we were confronted with the, at present, insuperable obstacles of the differences of race and culture; and our conclusion was, in effect, that if it is so outrageously difficult to establish decent human relations between members of the same race, it is almost impossible to conceive them as obtaining between two nations. In that case, again, no immediate remedy was possible, but it was suggested that we might at least make a beginning of by cultivating a friendly state of mind between ourselves and the Scandinavian Countries with the addition of Holland.

Our lecturer would then, no doubt, conclude with a well thought out peroration stressing the need for more and ever more co-operation between men of every degree and nationality commenting on the part that modern science will play in attaining that ideal— with a reference to Sir Josiah Stamp's presidential address at Blackpool to the members of the British Association—and ending with a prophetic picture of an ideal world something in the style of the various models submitted from time to time by H. G. Wells.

II

ALL that has been said in this cursory examination of the present state of man has regarded him simply as a space-time phenomenon. For the purpose of this objective survey I have treated him as a kind of superior animal capable of receiving a modicum of education, and within rather narrow limits, amenable to reason, taking those characteristics as representing the lowest common factor with which we could deal conveniently. The results so far have gone to show that the chances of founding a national, to say nothing of a world, Utopia are exceedingly remote. We have been confronted from the outset by the problem of man's diversity, of the enormous gulf that may separate the intellectual, moral and temperamental qualities of one man from another. And our ethico-sociological lecturer, following docilely in the footsteps of antecedent social reformers has sought his remedy for the ills of civilization by lessening these differences. If one man cannot understand another, lessen the differences between them by education. If two classes cannot live together in peace, lessen the differences between them by some plan of economic reconstruction. If two nations cannot agree lessen the differences between them by the encouragement of internationalism. Let us, in short, level up a bit and level down a bit until we

26

get an overwhelming majority of people in agreement upon certain broad principles of thought and conduct. Such principles should be easy to determine. They have been determined and accepted often enough in the past.

This seems and always has seemed, a straightforward solution of the sociologist's problem. Some reformers have laid more accent on levelling up, others on levelling down, in their working programmes. But, however various and incompatible their prescriptions may have been, they were substantially at one in their main endeavour to produce a static condition by striking a reasonable average and holding it up as a model. It has been the way of civilization, blindly and ignorantly followed, but still seeking to maintain an average of morality and good conduct by the imposition of laws defining what the members of any community may *not* do. It is, also, the way of those religions, whose object, broadly stated, is the raising of our moral and spiritual standards up to the level at which the congregation shall be able to pass its final examination after death.

What, then, are our objections, if any, to planning Utopia on the assumption that some such levelling is the inevitable condition of men living together in unity, always with the suggestion that we intend as far as possible to level up, and raise the standard as we go?

Let me answer that by saying in the first place that I believe the principle involved to be the right and the only one possible. It is the way of nature, and I believe it to be the way of the Eternal Purpose. Its goal is Unity, the final resolution of all diversity in that which our minds are too limited to conceive: God, the Everlasting Spirit, the One in the Many.

But having said that plainly and without qualification, I have to return to the question of method, and there I seem to be at odds with all the reformers inasmuch as I do not believe that our object can ever be attained by force. And by force I mean not only wars and bloody revolutions, but also, the imposition of laws, strict moral training, or even the offering of rewards and the threat of punishment, to be enjoyed or suffered after death. All these means may be necessary for the maintenance of civilization, but now we have left the sociological platform and are no longer considering man as the unit of a community. Instead of that he is assumed in all that follows, as a pilgrim soul having a past and a future outside the limitations of the three dimensional, temporal existence during which he is a fugitive among the illusions of material phenomena.

I propose to begin my argument against force, or compulsion by a descent into the rather muddy waters of psychology, taking an illustration from the effect of war experience on two representative types, contrastingly influenced by the exigencies of civilization.

The first is sensitive, ethically-minded, sympathetic. In peace-time, he is diligent and conscientious, an admirable employee so long as his work does not demand initiative. His tendency is towards introversion and he has few friends. He will never make a real success in life, and will probably marry a wife who will come to despise him for his inability to assert himself. What happens to him in war? If he gets through his earlier experience without becoming a case of war-neurosis, he will find his own release from the compulsions of civilization, the chief compulsion for him having been the need to assert himself. In the Army that need has almost ceased to exist, and he finds what he has always before lacked, communal life, real companionship. He and the men alongside of him are temporarily united. They have a common object. They share the same dangers and the same escapes from danger. They are under the same orders. And so for a time our Number One has a partial experience of that unity in co-operation which he could never find in his City office or his life in the suburbs. He will tell you, if you ask him, that war is horrible, loathsome, but that he found something in it which he has never known before or since. In his private thoughts, he will now and again forget all the horrors, and think of the war as the happiest time of his life.

Number Two has always had the making of a "rough," but has been restrained by social opinion and economic necessity. He has been in trouble once or twice as he becomes brutal when drunk, but except as a result of these outbreaks has kept out of prison. He makes a magnificent soldier when there is actual fighting to be done. At those times he is able to release all his repressions and take a real joy in brutal killing. After all those years of forced inhibition, he has civilisation's warrant for acting as a brute beast, and he takes the fullest advantage of it. But when that warrant is removed by the declaration of peace, he is unable to return to his old slavery. His is the type that has been responsible for so many murders and crimes of cruelty since the war. It is a type that appears to be even more common in the United States than in Great Britain. In many American film dramas it is held up for our admiration, as the hundred per cent "he-man."

Now it need hardly be explained why our Number Two can never be levelled up by compulsion to the lowest possible average necessary for a united society. We have to realize that the more inhibitions we lay upon him, the stronger become his unconscious resistances until the hidden force will overpower him and he would find even in Utopia, some such release as he found in the war. This is an exaggerated instance used as an illustration of the general psychological principle that all inhibitions imposed by the will lead to counteractions in the unconscious—one of the very few psychological principles that approach the validity of "laws." At present, we call it the "criminal type" and to the best of our ability prevent it from harming the community by incarcerating it in prisons and lunatic asylums.

Number One is not so easily accounted for, but we have seen that he has been unable to find any real happiness in our modern civilization. The real compulsion that has been laid upon him then is the need for competition, a need to which he has not enough extra vitality to respond. We should find a use for him in Utopia, but he would be very poor material for a revolutionist. He may make a good employee but he has a constitutional dislike for being compelled to do anything new or different. He is the kind that might decline a higher position if it necessitated a complete change of routine and more responsibility.

It is a queer comment on our present civilization that two such strongly contrasted psychological types should have found release in war. It may appear at first sight that they were put under a sterner discipline in the Army than was necessitated by the rules of civilization. But the Army discipline was only of the body, and most of it was positive. In the Army there were so many things they had to do. In civilization all the rules are negative. We are told, none too clearly and explicitly, what things we must not do and have to find our own ways to avoid them. In war our brutal Number Two could do just those things that civilization forbade. Our uninitiative Number One found himself the equal of his fellow men. Is it possible to obtain the same compensations for our two types in the building of our Utopia? What can we do to level them up to an acceptable average?

Let us turn aside for a moment to reconsider what Hitler has done in Germany. There to all appearances regimentation has produced a very fair imitation of unity, but the chief instrument employed has been the appeal to a highly-spiced nationalism. And as I said in an earlier paragraph, the majority of the younger generation in Germany were ripe for such an appeal. Could they possibly be conceived as responding to it, if they had not been? What has made the Nazi policy successful is not the force of compulsion but the presentation of an ideal to which so large a body of young German men was ready to respond. They have been led not driven. It is not regimentation that has succeeded but the lure of working together for a common cause, precisely the same kind of satisfaction that our Number One found in the Great War. And, if we can believe the reports, the young German Number Twos are able to find release for their inhibition in the treatment of political prisoners.

Have I now suggested an answer to the questions posed in the last paragraph but one? Is there in the world to-day any common ideal, strong enough to induce the nations of Europe to live together in peace and friendship? Or, if that be too far-distant a hope, is there any rallying cry that may lead the people of Great Britain in a common cause, the increase of goodwill among men? The earnest wish to sink personal ambitions and awards in the service of humanity?

III

EVERYONE knows the answer to that rhetorical question. Has a single generation passed in the course of the last nineteen hundred years, without the rediscovery by a few—sometimes by many—inspired individuals of the cure for all the ills of civilization? It is so simple. This new commandment I give unto you that ye love one another. We have but to do that and all our difficulties will instantly disappear. It is the very heart and soul of Christianity. Obey it and there will be no further need for what is now known as "religion." Sectarianism would become impossible, just as poverty, crime, self-seeking, pride, ambition and all the other deadly sins would become impossible. Can anyone doubt that if we all obeyed that one commandment, we should know a greater happiness than we can possibly know in modern conditions? Why, then, don't we all begin to-morrow and inaugurate the first year of the Millennium?

We don't because we can't. We don't love our neighbours and we do not want to. We have not the slightest wish even to try, and if we had we couldn't do it. That, if they were honest, and some of them would be, is the answer most people would return to us. A small minority might reply with equal sincerity that they were doing their best. Here and there we shall find one

33

whose best is very good. Nowhere shall we meet one who has reached the stage implied by the injunction; Be ye therefore perfect as your Father in Heaven is perfect. So, having taken that for granted, we can come to the level of common humanity and make some inquiry as to what we mean by love and why we are so woefully lacking in it.

We cannot, of course, define "love". It is one of those abstract words like life and consciousness which convey a definite idea in practice but whose essence is beyond the grasp of the finite mind. All such words relate to forces that are non-dimensional and non-temporal. We know nothing of them except in so far as we recognize their expression in this limited world of sensory experience. Wherefore the best we can do is to take the highest expression of love on this plane of existence and infer from that what we lack.

There is no need for us to attempt any picture of this highest expression for ourselves, as St. Paul has already done it fully and comprehendingly. And if we take his list of the attributes and test ourselves by it, we shall have to admit that we cannot find such love in ourselves nor have ever recognized it in others. To love like that demands an absolute selflessness and which of us is capable of that? This ideal love is all giving and no taking, and it is giving without the least ulterior thought of any return or reward whatever, either in this world or the world to come. But having admitted that such perfection is beyond our attainment, we must go back a step and inquire where we go astray. If, for example, we are incapable of loving all men, are we capable of feeling any approximation to such a love as this for any one human being, husband, wife, child, father, mother, or friend?

I doubt it. We may go a very long way towards it, but do we not always look for some return? Could we continue to lavish this abundance of selfless love on one who was faithless and indifferent? Shakespeare gave us a test when he said Love is not love that alters when it alteration finds, which is another way of saying that we are apt to seek in the loved one a conformation to some particular pattern we happen to admire. All such love has evidently too strong an element of self-satisfaction in it, one of the chief and most subtle rewards we are for ever seeking. We may, for instance, see what appears to be the selfless love of a mother for her son when she is willing to forgive him any fault, from whom she looks for no return, but before acclaiming hers as the perfect example, we must inquire whether that love is not all that she has to live for, her one satisfaction in life? And the discovery of any *reason* for love brings it down to another level. The kind of love we are discussing at the moment knows nothing of reasons or of reason. It is not of the mind but of the Spirit.

Wherefore, abandoning all counsels of perfection while never forgetting that perfection is our final aim, we may come down to the foot of the ladder which leads from earth to heaven; and from that lowly standpoint inquire what it is that primarily impedes us in the desired ascent. The answer is our egotism. From birth to death we are seeking some kind of satisfaction from our own beloved personalities. And we seek it, according to our various natures, in innumerable ways. At the lowest we seek it for our bodily cravings, food, drink, the appeasement of lust, ease, comfort, pleasure, excitement, all of them means of putting the mind to sleep. In a higher stage, it is the mind rather than the body to which we pander by indulging the control of the intellect. At the best we seek the satisfaction of the Spirit, or the approval of our own conscience.

This is, of course, a purely arbitrary classification. If we were to take the most extreme representative of any of these divisions we should find in him some influence of the wish to satisfy the demands of the other two classes of desires. No man can live for the satisfaction of his body alone, or of his mind alone, or of his Spirit alone. Wherefore our divisions represent differences of degree, not of kind; and there is no line of demarcation between one division and another. As seen by the eyes of the world, the eyes with which we are seeing in this examination, a man may step from what we have called the lowest to the highest division in a single hour as in cases of religious conversion. But all that concerns us here is the question of how this satisfaction of the personality, no matter what may be the predominant characteristic that enables us to classify it, stands between us and the attainment of our posited ideal.

It may be as well to begin by stating a truism that was implicit in the last paragraph, namely that no man can go on existing unless he can find some reason for pride in himself. The reason may be his excessive humility, but for him it is a cause for self-satisfaction. If we lose every source of satisfaction in the self, we die or become insane. With which statement we may turn our attention from extremes to the contemplation of our relations, friends, acquaintances, enemies, and the kind of people we meet every day.

And I do not think I can do that better than by putting what follows in the form of a personal statement. I, too, am one of these ordinary people, and anything I have to say about my fellows is no more than the result of sixty-three years of personal experience, prejudiced by this perpetual mandate to find a means of self-satisfaction. I am just as much biassed by that urgency as anyone else, and have, therefore, no excuse for speaking from platform or pulpit. My one possible claim upon you for a hearing is that I am conscious of my bias. Most people will strenuously deny the charge of prejudice.

The first accusation that I lay against myself and, I think, quite a preponderating majority of mankind is the desire to teach. Precisely what we teach will depend upon our individual make-up, the particular balance of qualities that we regard as constituting our own character. The root of this desire to teach lies in the desire to defend our own personality. Parents want to train their children on the same models as those which they have accepted, or been forced into, themselves. The models of the father and mother may not be the same, of course, and in that case the family will be an unhappy one, but whether the effort is united or not, does not effect our present purpose.

37

The essential thing is that the threat of departure by the children from the parent's standards is a direct attack upon them. If the parents are Christians and the child becomes agnostic, or vice versa, a criticism is levelled at the parent's beliefs. The instance is a peculiarly marked one, but any other will do as well, such as a threatened departure by the child from the parents' code of social respectability. In every case the effect is the same. The child is questioning those causes for self-satisfaction which its parents have chosen or been educated into believing, as the only right way of life. These beliefs have become the justification for their own precious personalities, and this defence of their beliefs is a defence of the self. And if that could be overthrown, the defender might in the last extreme, be robbed of his desire for life.

It becomes therefore, a settled habit with most of us to defend our own way of life by trying to teach it not only to our children but to the world at large. With the humbler people who have access to no public platforms, the desire is satisfied in a dozen small ways, some of which are not regarded as the attempt to teach but as the natural expression of an individual creed. But, fundamentally, every such expression whether among the humble or the proud, is traceable to the same source, the desire for self-justification. It is a desire that takes an immense diversity of forms, it may be exhibited as a will to reform the world, a pride in social respectability, the holding of any shade of political or religious opinion, but ultimately all these different variations of the will to teach are urged upon us by the inner need to exalt or defend our own personalities by making others like ourselves.

With those in whom the ability to teach is almost lacking, the satisfaction of this inner need is generally found by frequenting the company of those who on the whole agree with them. In such company they find the required justification for pride in their own opinions. Wherefore in this modern, diverse world, we have a host of queer sects and societies representing some little peculiarity that its members have in common, some idiosyncracy of faith or tendency that must be accounted as a virtue, if its owner is to live at peace with himself. If we cannot teach with our mouths, we can become the disciples of those who represent as nearly as may be our own opinions, and can preach them for us. By this means we obtain a vicarious satisfaction for the impulse to prove that ours can be the only right way.

George Moore, in "Abélard and Héloïse," says that the instinct of teaching is but the fruition of a man's belief in the truth of his ideas; but can we credit him with having chosen that elusive word "instinct" with scrupulous care? We may say that birds, for example, have an instinct for teaching their young, but no such natural gift is shown by human parents. If, however, I am right in the suggestion that teaching is an expression of the will to survive, Mr. Moore's use of the doubtful word may be claimed as a stroke of genius; for no instinct in humanity is so strong as that for self-preservation.

I put this teaching propensity of ours first in my

consideration of the obstacles that prevent our mounting the ladder "pitched between heaven and earth," because it covers so wide a range of human relations. But, although this propensity is obviously not the only expression of egotism, the other forms need not occupy us here. We know them all well enough. Greed, lust, pride, cruelty, hate and the rest, are so easily recognizable in our neighbours, and the traces of them excused in ourselves, that we may take it for granted that most people have some proportion of them included in their general make-up. Let us frankly admit that we are all egotists, and in making the admission take one step towards judging our fellow-egotists less critically. The beam may be in their eyes and the mote in our own, but if we are to mount from earth to heaven, it will be as well to treat the mote first. Christ, you will remember, was particularly severe in the matter of judging our fellow men.

I may so far, have seemed to regard this universal effort after some sort of self-justification as the simple fundamental impulse of our lives. But if that were true, this essay would conclude as it began, in a hopeless admission of materialism, seeing man as nothing more than a transitory phenomenon produced by some unknown and unrealizable Force. A little further consideration, however, will show that much of what has been said in this last section contains some evidence for the belief that man's being holds an immortal principle. For this effort after self-justification upon which I have insisted is not only a defence against the world but, also, against another inner urgency which prompts us to do things that are not apparently, in our own interests. Indeed this inner conflict often involves a greater effort than that needed to present an acceptable version of ourselves to the world.

This inner impulse, as I recognize it, is always towards some form of unselfishness, and for that reason is constantly repressed. Moreover, if it is obeyed in order to further our own interests, it soon ceases to influence us. It has something of that absolute quality we found in love, but as soon as we consciously seek to use it, it is translated into the terms of our ordinary social life. How then can we develop this precious seed of immortality, this secret gift which we believe to contain the potentialities of the perfection we are seeking?

It is there that every teacher, however great, must confess his weakness. For if there is one thing certain on this Earth, it is that no man or woman can be taught to love. No formula, no rules, ritual or dogma will avail us in this, nor even devotion to a deliberate practice. We may go about the world with the sincere determination to love our neighbours, we may be generous, patient, resolutely avoiding the speaking and thinking of evil. But although we may find great self-satisfaction in that practice and incidentally do much good to others, we shall not learn by practice the true meaning of love. Love is never deliberate or determined, nor, though it may wear that appearance to the world, patient, and long-suffering. It is spontaneous, effortless, and as has been said knows neither reasons nor reason. It is the gift of our immortality, the ex-

41

pression of the soul, and those who can realize it in its abundance know their immortality while they are still in the flesh and have the power to work what we call miracles. For faith is but a temporal aspect of love, and a means to win it, and that faith which shall move mountains does not come to us until it is merged in the greater power that makes man the vehicle of the all-powerful Spirit—to the potentialities of which, even over matter, we can assign no limit.

We have soared again into the empyrean, to the contemplation of perfection, but must return to the world for a further inquiry as to how we can find our way towards this immensely distant ideal, the only final solution of the problem of human relations. I have said dogmatically that love can neither be taught nor learned by assiduous practice. Is there any other way? Since we all have within us the seed of perfection how can it be brought to flower and fruit? That we are so wonderfully endowed we cannot doubt. Christ said the Kingdom of God is within you, and told us to seek it. But to do that we must in the first place have faith. We must believe absolutely that this gift of the power to love is something that we share not only with our fellow-men but with God. It is no good to seek it if we are not sure that it is there to be found. And the finding of faith is but one degree less difficult than the finding of love. For this search, also, demands the abandonment of reason, a complete submission of the intellect—that astounding machine which if it be fed with certain premises, derived from what we call the "facts" of observation and experience, is able to produce conclusions that are perfectly valid in their relation to the particular premises we have abstracted from the universal content. Wherefore faith founded on reason is only a form of mechanical belief, resting on premises which cannot be universal seeing that our knowledge of the universe is so severely limited.

Having, therefore, abandoned reason as an instrument of our search, how shall we find faith. Meditation and prayer are valuable aids, but they are not easily learned. We cannot, for example, meditate to any good effect, if we have not made friends with our own being—another immensely difficult task to be undertaken single-handed. While we are the battle-grounds of a perpetual conflict between our various "selves,"— and we have so many—true meditation is impossible. Somehow or other we must find a road to peace before we can come to any sight of that deeply hidden true self, the immortal principle, which contains the germ we are seeking.

And prayer presents much the same difficulties, though it may be used as an exercise towards the attainment of single-mindedness. To be truly effectual it, too, demands that vital element of faith, which seems to involve a vicious circle, from which we can, however, escape by limiting the nature of our prayer. We must in fact pray for something in which we can believe with all our various selves. If there be only one dissentient, one side of ourselves that stands apart in doubt, our faith will work no miracles. For to work miracles it is essential that our whole being should be in co-operation, a momentary unity, however evanescent. I do not believe, for example, that anyone can pray effectively for any selfish end. For to do that eliminates the co-operation of the one magic-working principle, the seed of perfect love which is what we are striving to reach. But if we can believe wholeheartedly that this immortal principle is there and pray for its expression through the mortal vehicle of our bodies, the constantly renewed statement of our wish will help to bring us peace. And if you ask to Whom you should pray, I say, pray to the God that is within you.

Finally, in this connection, there is that "wish" just referred to as the statement of our desire. It is the Wish not the Will that will serve us. Will is of the mind and negative. Will implies the enslaving of some of those various selves of ours, and they may one day revolt from bondage. Never, in any case, will these repressed selves give us willing service; and it has been assumed that we shall need their co-operation even in prayer. Wish, on the other hand, the wish for this gift of love is the positive expression of the spirit, of the inborn desire for unity; and if we can but wish long enough, and ardently enough, all our various selves will be drawn into the flame of longing after perfection. Wherefore, whenever, however transitorily, we find this wish for love in ourselves, we should rejoice in and encourage it, without too close an inquiry into its purity. Let us accept every wish to be the agent of Divine Love, as a sign from the heaven that is within us.

IV

THE exponents of sociology, psychology and religion have all expressed their views on this question of Human Relations, attempting to be as radical as the title of the volume exhorts them to be; and the general conclusions that may be drawn from what they have said are:

(1) Man is divided from man and nation from nation by innate diversities of temperament;

(2) Each individual is similarly divided against himself, a composite of opposing desires;

(3) There is but one way of escape from this perpetual conflict of diversities, which is so far beyond our immediate reach that the very Saints may hardly attain it.

The first and second of these statements are indisputable, the third is a question of faith and cannot be maintained by any logical argument.

But those who directly repudiate the third statement, and those who find the search after perfection beyond their powers, may still do something to save themselves and the world from the miseries of this diversity. So many people are now coming to the conclusion that there is something rotten in the state of our present civilization, that they should be willing to try so far as they are able to amend it. To do that it will be as well, in my opinion, to start with ourselves. The success of a society must be judged ultimately by the relations obtaining between its members. Where there is concord, where the members are working together, the society succeeds to the limit at which an opposing society will allow it to do so; wl ere there is discord the society is torn apart and ceas s to exist.

In the past this self-evident statement has begotten many proverbs, but in the past, the unit in which none was for a party and all were for the State, was always assumed as being defensive, or offensive, or both. In this essay the unit has been assumed as non-belligerent and world-wide, an assumption that rules out the compacting function of the unifying idea, since unless the exponent of statement No. 3 should happen to be right, there can be no unifying idea powerful enough to unite all the peoples of the world in a common object. Wherefore, having ruled out such temporary remedies for internal dissension as the appeal to patriotism and the making of wars, we have to create the conditions from which in generations to come the unifying idea may arise. And can that possibly be done unless we begin with ourselves? Is it not sufficiently obvious, and have not men of every condition been saying for generations past, that we shall never get Utopia or Socialism or peace until we get what is often called "a change of heart"?

And might it not be as well, even for our own sakes, to try to get it? We know perfectly well what stands in the way, our egotism: self-pride, intolerance of everyone who disagrees with us, the desire to convert others to

46

our own way of thinking, spite and vindictiveness, greed, the love of ease and comfort, every despised and unpleasant quality you can think of which may be used in some way or another to minister to our satisfaction in what we regard as our own precious personalities. It is this perpetual encouragement of ourselves in diversity, our obstinate refusal to recognize our likeness in others, which is the sole cause of the rottenness in civilization which we have done our best to bring about and now deplore. Would it not be worth while to make a small beginning by looking for the best in other people instead of the worst, by admitting now and again that our own opinions and those of the people who agree with us, are not necessarily the only right way of thinking? I cannot believe that we really prefer discord to harmony.

II
POLITICS
Lionel Birch

POLITICS

"POLITICS," in the very loose sense in which I propose to use the word in this essay, is the only available instrument through which ordinary people are supposed to be able to affect the shape of society according to their wishes. On the whole, politics to-day is used either as an instrument for keeping things more or less as they are, or as an instrument for altering things into something which is believed to be the better.

People who have no truck with politics presumably either do not care whether things alter or stay the same, or else they don't believe that politics have any power to alter or to preserve the existing shape of society.

If you are in the habit of believing that one kind of framework of society is better than another kind then, sooner or later, these days, you'll be reduced to taking part in politics. Even if you start off by believing that it's not the framework, but the people inside the framework that are decisive, even then, at this point of history, if you care enough for the people, you'll end up in some sort of politics. And once in, although you will be disgusted, and disillusioned and outraged time and again, you won't find it easy to get out. 1937 is a year in which it is necessary both to take sides oneself, and also to provoke other people to take sides, as well. To

51

refuse to take sides to-day is to commit a positive act of nullity, which, in the fullness of time, will ripen into active and general annihilation.

Politics is the only possible instrument through which we can ensure that the efforts of society are directed either towards the making of death or towards the making of life.

The fact that, in daily practice, "politics" is so often either a career, a ladder, a hobby, a drug, an exhibition, a half-conscious deception, or simply an opportunity for using other people's utterances as though they were your own bright ideas, does not affect the basic importance of politics.

That is why it is vital now that those people who are most likely to be shocked and repelled by the climbing and the mouthing should not abdicate from conscious participation in politics altogether. We may all, with the exception of some Duce or Inner Five, be forced to abdicate from politics soon enough. In the meanwhile, any abdication from the exercise of the distinctively human attribute of choice, gives some potential Inner Five a further reason for springing, fully armed, to birth.

Moreover, there is, in fact, no escape from politics. The life and the death of the most unrepentant non-voter are governed, in the last analysis, by politics. "The punishment wise men suffer, who refuse to take part in government, is to suffer under a government of worse men," said Plato. And from nine months before a man arrives into this land of Hope and Glory until the day when he passes out of it again, his happiness or his frustration, his opportunities, or his lack of them, his chances of an early death or a later, are determined chiefly by politics—whether he himself consciously participates in them, or whether he doesn't.

It is true that, up to a certain age, some people seem to have some armour against politics.

The walls which surrounded the garden of the place where I had the luck to be brought up, were very high. In summer you could hardly see the mellowness of the red brick for plums and pears and peaches, and fig trees seldom barren. In summer, when the herbaceous borders were at their proudest, and when there was no hunting or shooting to be done, one seldom went outside the place except perhaps to go and play tennis inside some other garden equally lovely.

The walls were perfect insulation. Sometimes on a still evening in February, you could hear the dog-foxes barking in the coverts, or the indignant screech of a cock-pheasant whirling up through the beeches in the Spring Coppice. There were few other sounds to be heard.

The day the War ended there were fireworks on the lawn and the groom set himself alight with a Roman candle.

One morning in 1926 we woke up to find that none of the morning papers had arrived. Around midday there appeared a strange-looking sheet called the *British Gazette*. Fortunately the chauffeur had a crystal set, so that it was possible to keep in touch with what was going on. And anyhow it was soon over, because, one gathered, it only took those Trade Unions ten days to come to their senses again.

Undoubtedly things used sometimes to happen in the outside world; but, when everything inside the garden had such harmony and tranquility, it would have seemed impertinent and superfluous to inquire too precisely into things which were not one's own immediate concern.

It is true that if you climbed the cotton tree by the lily pond on a clear spring morning you could just see where the sky was being stained by the smoke of the Black Country, not fifteen miles away. But, then, the Black Country was altogether a sinister land. Uncouth manufacturers issued out of it from time to time, and paid their subscriptions, and rode their horses on the tails of hounds and shot hen pheasants when they were sitting in fir trees.

The pity seemed to be that one ever had to leave the walled garden. For, from the windows of the school train, it was impossible not to catch a glimpse of the thousands of burning slag heaps and the rows of grey houses looking like the stables at home, which passed for the countryside between Wolverhampton and Birmingham.

Of my prep. school I remember chiefly two questions asked by the boy who shared my double-desk in form. The first question was about babies. The second was: "Please, sir, what's a Conservative?" The form-master, who had been a little rattled by the first question, made short work of the second: "Everyone's a Conservative," he said, "unless there's something very peculiar about them." And I, who was in a sweat of anxiety lest there should be anything peculiar about *me*, became a Conservative on the spot. The following holidays I won my spurs. In the local bye-election I sat next to the chauffeur while he was picking up voters, and on the way to the poll, I promised them each the agonies of the damned and the punishments of the very peculiar, if they failed to vote "the right way".

I remember at my public school feeling particularly scandalized at the sight of a single master wearing a Labour rosette during the 1928 election. Nor shall I forget learning history from the recognized history books.

By the time of the 1931 election I was at Cambridge. Being twenty-one years of age, I had attained full citizenship. It was certain that I was entitled to a vote, but it appeared that something had happened to it. Anyhow, I couldn't use it at Cambridge. If I had been able to use it, I should probably have voted against the Conservative candidate, because I disliked the face and manner of the Conservative canvasser.

On the other hand, one never knows. Most of the papers were saying that if the Socialists got in again the Pound would fall, and I particularly wanted to go to Germany in the Long vacation, and knew just enough about economics to realize that if the Pound fell, my holiday abroad would cost me more. In any case, I had a feeling that the mislaying of my vote was of no great consequence, and that, if this was all citizenship consisted of, I couldn't for the life of me see why people had in the past paid such large sums to become citizens.

5

On the other hand, the fact that, before the election, all the papers were saying that it would be disastrous if the Pound went off gold, whereas after the election, when the Pound had gone off gold, all the papers were saying that it was the best thing that had ever happened —this fact induced me to devote my last year at Cambridge to "reading" economics.

In June 1932, I stood on the steps of the Senate House in dinner jacket, white tie and white furry hood, a consummate Bachelor of Art, and as much in the dark as it was possible to be. There we all were, crowds of healthy looking young men, loitering around Cambridge on Degree Day, twiddling our "squares" and wondering what was supposed to happen next.

And what did happen next to all these scholar-athletes and Bachelors of Art, on whom so much progress, enlightenment and tradition had been sprayed, and in whom so much capital had been sunk? Some of them, a small proportion, packed their bags and, after a fortnight in Paris, went off to start paying their dividends at once. Every year a certain proportion of the youth of the country is thrown to the new Minotaur, is put into The Office, so that a dead civilization may not have to lie down quite yet. The survivors, those on whom the lot has not fallen to be herded into the Labyrinth, wander around London or the Continent for a time, honestly believing that, if they are allowed to do nothing for a bit longer, they really will be able to do something. At the other end of the scale, the other unemployed are wiser. They know that if they do nothing for a bit longer they will soon really be able to do nothing at all. The patient gentlemen of England.

Eventually, one supposed, some of the unemployed University Graduates would trail back to their own, or other people's, preparatory or public schools. Having failed to make any sense of their own lives, they would proceed to mess up other people's in advance. They would return, mangled still further, to their old frame, to scrape a living by educating the young for life. For what life? Don't ask silly questions, daft and gentle reader.

Anyhow, there was I, walking about Cambridge in fancy dress one morning in June 1932, trying to ask myself the question "What am I going to *do*?"

What was I going to do, firstly, to keep myself alive? Secondly, what was I going to do to satisfy myself that life and my contribution to it were at all worth while?

There were certain things I was probably qualified to do in order merely to keep myself alive. I could probably have become a schoolmaster, or a soldier, or a parson, or a stockbroker, or a solicitor, or a barrister, or a chartered accountant, or a bank clerk or an estate agent. On the other hand, I could not persuade myself that, in any of these professions, I should feel that I was making any very useful contribution to things in general. I do not know why I felt that these professions were futile and irrelevant. I simply was convinced that they were so.

Unable to find any satisfactory solution to this dilemma, I went into a public bar. Possibly, I thought,

57

with the aid of enough beer and whisky one might come to feel that a life devoted exclusively to buying and selling stocks and shares, was in reality serving some divine, or at least some useful, purpose. It was twelve o'clock, and some men from a building job that was going on behind the Town Hall were eating their bread and cheese at the table. I remembered how, when I was much younger, I had read a sentence from Adam Smith to the effect that "Labour is the source of all wealth." When I had asked the nearest elderly relation how, if labour was the source of all wealth, it came about that all the people in the village who worked hard seemed to be quite poor, while all the people who were rich in the village didn't seem to do anything at all, the nearest elderly relation duly answered: "Don't ask silly questions."

A conviction now seized on me that the foregoing inscrutable mystery and the immediate question "What am I going to do that I can feel to be worth while?" must be in some way intimately related.

The subsequent investigation of that relationship has provided the substance for this essay on politics.

Up to the year 1900 or thereabouts, politics, as I now see it, consisted fundamentally of a struggle between two rival groups of would-be exploiters. Since 1900, politics has consisted of a struggle between the two rapidly coalescing groups of exploiters on the one hand, and the exploited on the other. It's only in the last forty years that the exploited have come into the political picture at all.

This, of course, is a very crude way of describing the situation. The old struggle between the two rival groups of exploiters was very keen; the development of long distance transport and navigation, together with the natural richness of this country had combined to make the prizes the largest in history. The English early bird of exploitation had two separate and distinctive worms—the English worm and the Asiatic worm. The prosperity of the governing classes in the roaring eighties was achieved at the expense of innumerable English working men, women and children, who were regimented into the production of cheap goods with which the new gods of Manchester were able to annihilate, at a stupendous profit, the craftsmen of India and China. In high glee, Oldham manufacturers tumbled over each other to sell their textile machinery to Japan. God was in his machine; all was right with the world.

Had it not been for the War—a war which was itself a product of this struggle for industrial supremacy—things might still have been more or less all right with the world. But, by 1920, it was seen that, amongst other things, the wheels of the machinery sold so gaily and so profitably to the Japanese, were beginning to go round.

The Japanese worm had turned, and was adopting some bird-like practices. The English worm was turning too. Indeed Lord Rothermere expressed his amazement at the rapidity of the growth of the English working-class movements of this time. It is true that simultaneously faithful Marxists expressed their amazement at the unpredicted slowness of its growth; a slowness which may have been due, in part, to the fact that some of the worms did not really want to change the whole basis of the bird and worm society, but merely wanted to be birds instead of worms. (Worm into bird. Subsequently, in 1931, we saw some shining examples of this phenomenon).

Anyhow, by 1920, the new line-up was pretty clear. Instead of two rival groups of oppressors squaring up to each other above the insensible bulk of their victim, the people who worked but did not earn coming into line opposite the people who "earned" but did not do any equivalent work. There the alignment stands to-day; the class struggle, the thing which conservatives delight to call the "class war," thereby conveying the impression that it is the working class which is the invading, combative party, and that the governing class are purely passive and reluctant defenders of their rightful province. Poor little Japan.[1]

The exploiters, the governing classes, by the way, are not ogres. In normal times their oppressions are purely incidental. But they are born differently, and they live so differently to the total number of members of other classes, that consequently they think in an altogether different way. And their opinions of what is for the best for everyone, though almost always

[1]"The Japanese are fully convinced that the action of the Japanese army on the night of September 18th 1931, and thereafter has never exceeded the limits appropriate to measures of self-defence, and that Manchukuo has been founded by the spontaneous will of the people of Manchuria." Official statement issued to members of the League of Nations. (c.f. Statements of National Govt. Spokesmen on the "Incitement to Disaffection Act" and similar invasions.)

sincere, are almost always "refracted" by their own exceptional way of living.

Even the proprietors of child-labour in the seventies of last century were not ogres by intention. They were in a position of advantage which they intended to hold against rival exploiters. Through their ownership of the means of production they were able to claim ownership of the whole of the finished goods produced by the labour which they employed. They bought their labour as they bought their raw materials—in the cheapest market. Each week the labour paid for itself—and for a good deal besides. Each week that good deal else, the value of the whole remaining product, went to the owners. Nothing intentionally ogreish in that. As yet the position of the owners was unchallenged, unless it happened to be challenged in a friendly way by other owners who thought that ownership in general would do better under Protection or under Free Trade, whichever it happened to be.

There are two main results of bird-and-worm politics. In the first place only about half of what might be produced is, in fact, produced. In the second place, the wretched amount that is produced is distributed in a wholly cock-eyed way. The actualities of the whole world lag miserably behind the potentialities; and, out of those puny actualities the people who do the jobs don't even get what they ought.

"Don't ask silly questions," said the nearest elderly relation.

And that is still the answer of the Press, the Radio, the Cinema and the Paternal State to anyone who is inquisitive enough to want to know why the people who work can work themselves into old-age without getting any security or any wealth at all, and why the people who are well off can be rich and secure without doing a hand's turn from the cradle to the grave.

"Don't ask silly questions." Of course, it's the only safe answer. Because the reason for this phenomenon, if it became sufficiently widely known, would soon cause people to turn things upside down, or, as I should prefer to say, would soon cause them to put things the right way up.

The reason is that, as we shall see in a moment, the way you are going to be fixed throughout your life is decided before you are born. Either you are going to be one of the owners, —the owners of land, or mines, or factories, or machinery (mechanical or human); or else you are going to be one of the owned, one of the bits of machinery (human), in fact. If you are going to be one of the owned, then, in the fullness of time, you, as a piece of machinery (human) will receive throughout the weeks of your working life, your oil and fuel (human); you will receive from week to week, in the form of wages, just enough to keep you in running order. Perhaps you will find a machine-owner who treats you well, with the same sort of caressive solicitude as that with which some working garage proprietors treat their cars. In due course, however, and in any case when you have worked your guts out and when newer and more up-to-date machines are available, you will have to be pensioned off with the best will in the world and with ten shillings a week on which to indulge in riotous living.

If, on the other hand, you are going to be one of the owners, of land, of mines or of machinery (mechanical or human) then, in the fullness of time, you will receive for your effort, or lack of it, all the values created that remain over after the monies due for raw materials and oil and fuel (mechanical and human) have been paid out. The chances are that, in a good year, a fair amount will remain over. And so you will live aloft in the village, comfortable without effort, rich without earning, and a source of inscrutable mystery to inquisitive small boys. And, for just so long as good-mannered little boys and the good-mannered public accept the elderly relation's answer "Don't ask silly questions"—for just so long you will continue to live in this way.

The results of bird-and-worm politics are, firstly, under-production (as well as under-consumption) and, secondly, maldistribution (as well as under-distribution). The net effect of these results is to make a fool of men's lives.

In course of time, however, a dual challenge began to make itself felt. On the one side this came from the owners of other countries, particularly in the East, who had been learning the tricks of the trade from willing, if short-sighted, English teachers. On the other side, the challenge came from home; but not, this time, from friendly rivals who thought they knew a better way of managing things. This challenge came from the hitherto inarticulate exploited ones, who had come to feel that, relative to the much greater material possibilities, not half enough was being produced, and that they themselves were not getting their share even of that not-half-enough production. This complaint revealed the tug-of-war that lies at the core of a society in which instruments of production are privately owned. The two sides were compelled, for the first time, to "take the strain."

The wage-earners demand higher wages; but, from the point of view of the shareholders, wages are simply a cost. And, if costs rise, there is less for the shareholders. Consequently, the directors, however benevolent they may be, feel bound to resist these demands, otherwise the shareholders will shout at them at the annual meeting.

In the early stages of the challenge, the owners were generally prepared, and able, to make concessions as the price of having a little peace. This is all right as long as capitalism is expanding. The concessions can be afforded without the owners noting much difference. But when foreign owners have made up their leeway, and there is little more chance of expansion, and there is not any immediate prospect of war, the situation begins to look ugly. When expansion ceases, but the gap between *what is* and *what might be* remains, a higher price has to be paid in the way of concession to the wage-earner. Then it is no longer a matter of the directors being shouted at in annual meetings but of the directors "not being able to keep the industry afloat."

When this condition becomes general, and when

wage-earners persist in their demands, the choice for the owners as a whole is between coercion and one last desperate concession. At this point, the more sensitive section of the owners becomes interested in Monetary Reform and probably propose a National Dividend. The more hard-boiled section becomes interested in rationalization, efficiency, coercion and the totalitarian and corporate states. When the practitioners of this last say that they have eliminated class war, they probably mean that they think they have eliminated the tug-of-war which lies at the core of a private ownership system. But they haven't done this. All that they have done is to replace the jostling team of owners by a few hefty individuals of double the normal weight, and to forbid the wage-earners' team to do anything other than go through the motions of tugging, on pain of being clapped into gaol. It is only in this last stage that owners become intentionally ogreish. There is now a significant body of opinion growing up which holds that there should now be a new alignment. That is to say Capital and Labour against "Finance"— whatever may be the precise meaning of that term. Whatever the alignment that ought to exist, the alignment which does exist is the alignment of the owners against the non-owners, with the owners much more on the offensive than they like people to believe. As Lord Esher remarked: "It never seems to occur to the Socialists that their ideas of the class war and the dictatorship of the proletariat can be copied by other classes more powerful than themselves." Lord Esher does not seem to have been referring merely to a sinister group of international financiers. The English owning classes may be peculiar, but they are not fools; and they have great *esprit de corps*.

Since 1900 politics may have appeared to have been about Protection, Free Trade, Alliances, Balances of Power, Treaties, preparation for the Great War for Civilization, Reparations for same, Hanging the Kaiser, War Debts, Covenants, Fascism, Slumps, financial crises, Nazism, Nationalization, and preparation for the next Great War of the Unemployed. In reality, those are all aspects of the same thing, i.e., the difficulty of agreement in external affairs between the early bird and the later, as to the equitable sharing out of worms, and, both externally and internally, the now manifested and impudent tendency of worms to turn.

To this may be added the suspicion beginning to be felt by people of all classes that it may not be possible for very much longer to conduct the world on a bird-and-worm basis.

Since 1929, moreover, the growing divergence between the obvious material potentialities and the evident miserable actualities has become alarmingly noticeable. And politics, since 1931, have consisted largely of efforts, dictated by fear, to prevent too many people realizing this divergence. With unerring instinct, for instance, the National Government has passed the Sedition Bill, so as to be able to clap into prison immediately anyone attempting to point out this divergence to the Armed Forces of the Crown.

Worms in Uniform! You, at any rate, shall not be allowed to turn!

"Labour, Art, Worship and Love—these make men's lives." And such everyday things as people going short of food while food is destroyed, and cowmen's children drinking tinned milk, and men being forbidden to work at all while other men are working fifty hours a week, and families being subjected to the stupidities and degradations of the Mean's Test—these things make a fool of men's lives. These things, while they remain, make nonsense of God and Nature.

Week by week, year by year, the things produced from the earth are distributed in predestined proportions. As they flow out from nature they are diverted into carefully separated channels—a comparatively spacious channel for the owners, a cramped channel for the owned. A weekly wage of, say, thirty-one shillings for the farm-worker, a weekly dividend of, say, thirteen pounds for the landowner. This process has been going on undisturbed for many years, and the strata are now well defined. It is this never-ending distribution flow which moulds society—the city and the town and the village—into layers. It is this which has shaped for us our stratified society, our society divided into non-competing groups, from one layer of which to the next layer up there is no ladder and no spring-board at all.

I happened at one time to spend a good many years near to a town which perfectly symbolized this stratification. In the top stratum—in the Queen Anne country houses on the hills above the town—lived the old county families and the families whose money had been made by a sufficiently far-distant ancestor to permit the county families to accept them. There they lived with their Hunt Balls, their cricket weeks, their shooting parties and their occasional dips into the Claridges-Ascot cycle. Verily they had their reward. Next, in the choicest parts of what was known as the "High Town" itself lived the professional classes with their own particular ring of tennis parties, bridge parties, saloon bars and so forth.

In the more work-a-day parts of the high town lived the shopkeepers and tradesmen, discerning men, trained in the perception of *nuances* and capable of distinguishing at sight between members of the two previous classes enumerated. Finally, in the "Low Town," separated by a sharp precipice from the comparative gods in the next layer up, lived the artisans, down in the reeds by the river, with the yellow mist perpetually rubbing its back against their window panes and with Father Severn coming to pay a call every now and then of a February.

All these different grades of people knew their places; and when they met, as they did sometimes, at church or out hunting, they knew how to greet each other with the emphasis appropriate to their respective strata. They were non-competing groups; and so long as they all remained non-competing they treated each other quite civilly across their dividing gulfs. The trouble began when some successful and hard-working manufacturer or industrialist came and bought one of the country houses on the hill, the daughter of which had failed to bring in a presentable American or other wealthy partner to keep the old place from going to pot. Whenever the people in the top stratum began vocally regretting "these democratic days," it usually meant that some hard-working industrialist had arrived with his spring-board—his filthy money—and was about to make a bid, literally, for entry into the top stratum. Whereupon the people in the top stratum would be able to get their own back by making comments about the new arrivals in the presence of their chauffeurs, butlers, grooms, etc.; and by being specially cordial to keepers, gardeners and cowmen who had no spring-board out of *their* layer, and who could therefore never possibly compete.

No doubt it's much the same in most counties. I remember going last Christmas, to a party, somewhere in Mayfair, at which I didn't recognize anybody at all.

"Do you know Hampshire?" I gambitted to a good-looking young man who happened to be nearest me.

"Very well," he said pleasantly. "I used to hunt regularly with the H.H. at one time, and I nearly always went down to Winchester for the partridges in September when I was up at Oxford. I seldom missed the H.H. Ball. Friends of mine had a place near Christchurch. Used to go down there a lot. Had some very good cricket. I got very fond of that country. Charming villages. Good people too."

The next day, driving out of London, I gave a lift to a man who waved at me on the Kingston By-Pass. "Going down there, are you?" he said, when I told him my destination. "Why" I asked, "do you know Hampshire?" "Do I know it?" he said. "Oh dear, Oh Lor! Why the wife and kids are living there at this day. I was a carter down there, onetime. Got stood off after 1929, look. Went on the parish for a while and got brought up to the beaks for taking a rabbit or two. Went down Southampton way with a poling firm, elevenpence an hour. When the job packed up, I'd got my stamps, and went on the Labour. After that I had a straight run through; P.A.C., Court of Referees, vacant ticket, and here we are again. I'd got round most of the county by the end of that time, look. Do I know Hampshire!"

We stopped to have a drink, and one of the men in the Public Bar began to join in our conversation.

"I suppose you know Hampshire, too," I said to him.

"Which Hampshire?" he retorted, "I know several of 'em." It was only later that I discovered that he was a bit drunk.

No doubt it's the same sort of thing in the cities, except that they are generally less organic entities, anyhow. Still, if you take a walk in London with your eyes open from Belgrave Square, through Eccleston Square and Warwick Street down to Lupus Street you'll notice that you've passed through almost as many different strata as it's taken you minutes to walk.

In a way, it's more serious in the cities; because the predestination seems to be more complete. Besides, not only are the gulfs between the strata strictly demarcated, but you can never be sure that there won't be a gulf between yourself and your neighbour, or rather the fellow who lives next door to you in the same street-stratum. Yes; it's even more remarkable in the cities, this "separateness of each man in his lair." And if a society divided against itself cannot stand, then what hopes on earth are there for a society such as ours which is not only inevitably slashed into several horizontal slices, but which has also submitted to having itself chopped up in a vertical direction as well?

But it is the predestination which is the portentous thing, when you realize its implications:—the fact that from nine months before you appear in the world as a separate entity your fate is sealed; and that, wriggle as you may, it is a hundred thousand to one against your ever emerging out of that stratum unto which it has pleased God to call you.

The life-progress of an individual may be regarded as a series of stages away from the perfect shelter: a period of poise: and then the longest journey back again. The womb represents both shelter, security and delegation of responsibility. The child emerges and is nursed; he has shelter, though with an occasional draught. He goes to school; still shelter, but considerably more draughts. Security of a sort, until he has left school, is guaranteed by the state. The state says "Thou shalt have schooling. And we don't want you dead on our hands." The first significant thing is that the state stops saying this at different times to the members of different strata.

If you give me the address of a foetus in a womb in any one street in London, I will tell you at what age it will finally emerge from shelter. A foetus in a street in Rotherhithe? That will finally emerge at the age of fourteen from an elementary school. A foetus in Park Lane? That will emerge at the age of twenty-two, from one of the Universities. One could safely elaborate these stunning predictions, forecasting the situation of each foetus at the ages of thirty, forty, fifty and so on. For the fact of the matter is, that, long before you're born, the whole of your future life-pattern is cut and dried. There are virtually no step-ladders up from a low stratum to a higher one, and you have to be outstandingly dissolute or outstandingly honest to be presented with a step-ladder down. The foetus which is going to be born in Rotherhithe is foredoomed. So, incidentally, is the foetus which is going to be born in Park Lane; only its doom is not quite so obvious.

In this way it comes about that in, say, Belgrave Square a child not yet born can actually own a million pounds, while in Warwick Street, a few hundred yards away, a woman who has worked all her life from seven to seventy is carried out to die in the workhouse.

We said that the child which is going to be born in a street in Rotherhithe is foredoomed. Foredoomed to what? Foredoomed to emerge as a human being into a world in which it can only have its labour to sell. But, in the world of 1935, there is no certainty that it will be able to sell its labour, even if it prices it as low as sixpence an hour. Approximately every fourth foetus in wombs situated in streets near Rotherhithe is *predestined* to be unable to sell its labour for enough money to keep body and soul together. Every fourth Rotherhithe foetus therefore is probably predestined to be compelled to sell its body in order to keep body and soul together.

It should be unnecessary to underline the fact that

every fourth Rotherhithe foetus is predestined to be arrested, dragged into court and sentenced for trying to sell the only saleable commodity which society still permits it to possess.

The prostitute of the street-walker type may or may not be naturally fastidious. Economic conditions simply do not in practice permit of fastidiousness. Two out of every three English prostitutes, says an eminent French woman journalist, are not "professionals," but underpaid or sweated working women and girls.

The prostitute is impelled by the refinements of poverty to sell her body for money. The majority of other professions elect (without the compulsion of conclusive poverty) to sell their psyches for money.

The Kensington criterion places the prostitute at the bottom of the social scale. Leaving aside, for the moment, the element of envy and morbid interest involved in this judgment, the reason given for it would probably be that the prostitute is absolutely unparticular as to what she does for a living. The implication is that Kensingtonians, on the other hand, are tremendously particular as to what they do for a living. As an elderly "friend of the family" said to me when I left Cambridge "So you are going to teach in one of these elementary schools? Well, no doubt that is a good thing in its way. But with your ability, my boy, we were all ambitious for you. We had hoped that you might become a chartered accountant, or a soldier, or a stockbroker like myself."

The Kensington or Park Lane foetus, as we have

73

observed, is not quite so obviously foredoomed. It is predestined to emerge into a world in which it will have not only its labour, but also its accent, its visiting card, its club ties, its healthy complexion, its "degrees" and all its other adhesive assets to sell. Sometimes, of course, its life will have already been mortgaged for it by its parents. ("Now, my boy, I have sunk £2,000 of capital in your education. It's time you paid a dividend.") It is likely, however, that every second Park Lane foetus, shall we say, is predestined to elect of its own (comparatively) free will to sell not only the aforesaid assets, but also its psyche, in order to obtain Security Plus. (Plus what? Plus that little something which enables one to have a "good time.").

The people concerned, and some others, may vehemently deny that participation in any of the usual Kensington professions involves selling their psyches; they may affirm that it is possible to be a chartered accountant, a soldier, a stockbroker, a parson, a solicitor, schoolmaster etc., and yet still call your soul your own.

No doubt it can be, and sometimes it is, done. But the people who do it have to be pretty robust, and they have to be prepared to withstand unceasing boycott and blackmail at the hands of the orthodox.

There is, moreover, no doubt that a large number of people who are forced to adopt one of these professions feel that they cannot call their souls their own, and are convinced that they are being forced to make a contribution to the bolstering up of a system which is putrid and mushy at the root. "Birth, Prostitution and Death."

74

Similarly there is no doubt that many street walkers don't think much of prostitution as a way of life. But "you gotta live."

Things are harder for the prostitute than the professional man, because the law frowns on people who try to sell their bodies in the short-term market. The law doesn't mind how many times a day you sell your soul; nor does it mind if you sell your body in the long term market. It periodically arrests the prostitute, but it invariably lets the debutante go scot-free. It is apparently almost a matter of routine that at least a dozen prostitutes should be arrested in certain London areas each night, for subsequent presentation at court. (Police court, of course). How much less cock-eyed it would be if a dozen debutantes were arrested each night of the season, for subsequent presentation at Bow Street. For why? For such disgusting vulgarity as would make a prostitute blush. After all, the prostitute in search of a bare living is quiet, orderly and modest. The debutante in search of Security Plus is flagrant, self-advertising and pornographic—altogether more demoralising to public modesty. Nor can it be assumed that it is merely the money transaction which makes the prostitute's behaviour disreputable. The man who picks up a well-advertised deb. is almost certain to have to pay over any amount of cash. Indeed, before the American boom broke in 1929, English debutantes were fetching the most fantastic prices.

We are all prostitutes now. Let him that is without a trace of prostitution in him first clap the handcuffs

75

on the woman taken in an attempt to earn her living. And let the magistrate who is without sin suggest to her an alternative way of earning it.

It is difficult to know what to make of magistrates who fine a woman ten shillings for accosting and tell her to go away and behave herself in future; or who sentence a man to one day's imprisonment for begging and tell him to clear out of the town and take care not to beg any more. What, one wonders, do magistrates expect these people to do? Are they supposed to go and live on air and acorns? Or simply and conveniently to fade away? Or to join the army and enjoy a man's life?

Consider, for a moment, this "man's life." Consider the soldier: the professional soldier, not the man who volunteers for some specific and known purpose. The professional soldier binds himself in advance to be hired out for any purpose for which his superiors may think fit to use him. He delegates his moral responsibility. He abdicates from his right to choose. He may be required to use poison gas against his German cousins, to break a strike on the part of his British cousins, to secure an Egyptian or an Austrian loan, or to go and protect British women, children and dividends in Shanghai. In all these matters he has no choice as to whether he will do it or not. In the words of the poet "Theirs not to reason why."

In some way the prostitute is in a more dignified position. It is open to her to reject a client if her daemon or her inclination impel her to do so. A large number of prostitutes reject each and every client for a large number of weeks on end. She still has some element of option left to her.

True, disgusting things happen in brothels. Remarkable things also, happen in Officers' Training Establishments; as witness this report of a lecture given by a company sergeant-major to the Inns of Court Training Corps in July 1918. The sergeant-major was speaking on the spirit of the bayonet.

"It was a good thing to show the Tommy how to kill a Boche and to get that delightful feeling of putting him out with a bayonet" he said, "to feel that he had finished off one of those dirty creatures that we call Germans . . .

"You will certainly know what it feels like to drive that bayonet home, and get it out again. You will feel that you will like to go on killing . . .

"If you see a wounded German shove him out and have no nonsense about it. What is the use of a wounded German anyway? Kill them, every mother's son of them. Exterminate the vile creatures! When a German says "Kamerad" you know that he wants to be put out of his agony." (Laughter).

At the end of the lecture an officer advised the training corps to bear in mind what had been said, and added the hope that "You will all try and act up to it."

All this is specifically not to cast aspersions on the qualities of soldiers as individuals. There are innumerable brave soldiers, for instance. There are many heroic prostitutes.

It is against the purpose to which these qualities are put that the present remarks are directed.

For the children of the working-classes the pre-destiny of a servile life; for the children of the middle-classes the predestiny of a venal one. To the young navvy the order is: "Sell your labour at the price which the owner thinks he can afford to pay, or starve." For the young man in the street: "Find some work however parasitic and futile, or starve." "Prostitute yourself, or starve." So much for the woman in the street; and precisely so much, also, for the artist.

Servility and prostitution are intermediate effects of the way in which productive and creative work is organized in our present society. The ultimate effect is War. The sequence is as follows: Divorce of each emergent individual from a rightful access to the means of productive or creative work—Servility and Prostitution—War. It is an eerie testimonial to the present system that war is the only apparent solvent for the frustrations which that system produces. The Unemployment problem solved! A paid job for everyone! Production struggling to keep up with a titanic consumption! Class war abolished! It all sounds rather like a set of Fascist election promises.

To anyone who agrees that military war is not an epidemic, but that it is only one inevitable stage in the permanent economic war which is endemic to the system, a pacifism which begins to operate merely at the outbreak of military operations may well seem to start in the middle and get nowhere. If we want to stop war we shall have to begin at the beginning, before the brass bands, before the prostitution and the servility, at the point where the declaration of economic war is made by the exclusion of the ordinary man from access to the means of work.

The economic war is caused by unceasing attempts on the part, successively, of unemployed men, employed men, foremen, firms of manufacturers, firms of distributors, firms of exporters, and, finally, exporting nations to cut in on the process of production which is not, as things are, large enough to accommodate them all.

It is like one of those American dances in which relays of men cut in on other men for the most favoured partners. In the present organization of society only a small proportion of available men can dance with Madam Industry at one time. The rest go, automatically, to the wall.

One man's meat is another man's meatlessness. One man's, or one firm's, or one nation's job is another man's or another firm's, or another nation's unemployment.

And the war of man against man outside a Labour Exchange for a job is only the first stage in an inexorable process which ends with the war of one nation against another for an export market.

"Because capitalism creates poverty at home, it is forced to seek for riches abroad. It makes the Dreadnought because it made the slum."[1]

Allow people to abolish the slum and the drop in the "Defence" Estimates will be amazing.

[1]H. N. Brailsford: "Socialism for To-Day"

"The world is trying to get peace at the same time as it is pursuing a policy which is known to lead to war. The world is trying to get peace on the cheap. It wants all the benefits of Christianity and at the same time to reject the cardinal doctrine on which Christianity is founded.

"Conscientious objection is poor stuff: it is un-principled in so far as it is based on a negation. We need to go deeper and discover a faith of which Pacifism is only one expression."[1]

We need to start our pacifism where the war process starts. Where does it start? Where is the seed of the thing which blossoms eventually into Passchendaele?

The seeds of war are in every factory and in every farm. We reap what we have sown. It is illogical and ineffective to refuse to reap. What we have to do is to sow differently. It is no use saying "No" to the blood-ripe harvest. We have to say "No" earlier, to the man who tries to sell us the same old seed.

Let us take a look at the business of Production and Distribution in farm and factory.

Two facts stand out at the present time.

1. An enormous and unparalleled capacity to produce goods.

2. A completely inadequate distribution of goods.

This however is not equivalent to saying (as Social Creditors say) that the productive system is alright and only the distributive system is wrong.

There are two common kinds of critics of the so-called

[1] Max Plowman in "The Adelphi"

paradox of poverty in the midst of plenty. One looks
at the situation and notices that not all the goods are
distributed which might be. The other notices that the
goods which are distributed are distributed very
inequitably.

The first view is concerned with what is true. The
second with what is just. They represent roughly the
mathematical and ethical views respectively of the
present deadlock.

The root-principle of the real economy of nature is
that production is the only authorization and enable-
ment to consume.

In the Garden of Eden, if Adam wanted to consume,
to eat, all he had to do was to go and plant and dig a
potato. That was the only authorization he needed to
consume, i.e., that he should produce.

To-day there are many millions of men who would
like to consume more than they do. They are, as things
stand, unable to do so. What has intervened, since
Adam and us, to prevent them? The mathematical
critic holds that an artificial thing called money has
intervened. As production became more complicated
money was devised as a convenient means of distribution. The making of the means of distribution has been
collared, since Adam's day, by "sinister individuals
who refuse to make enough." Hence the millions are
prevented from consuming because they have no
money, because there are not enough tickets. The
population is divided into those who have enough
money and those who have no money.

The ethical critic holds, on the other hand, that the

thing which has intervened between Adam and us, is the theft, not of the means of making money, but of the land and resources, which prevents men who wish to consume from doing so. For Adam, the only authorization needed to consume was that he should produce. For the millions of Englishmen to-day the authorization to consume is more complicated. They cannot go straight to the land and plant and dig a potato. Because the land belongs to private persons. The authorization to consume is not to go to the land and dig; but to go to the landlord and ask permission to dig, on his terms. The landlord's (or the factory-owner's) terms are as tight as they can be. They involve the surrendering of everything produced to the owner of the land or factory, and the return to the worker of only so much as will keep him just alive. The population is divided into those who own the instruments of production and those who do not own them; who therefore cannot produce; and who therefore have no natural authorization to consume.

In England the working population was divorced from access to the means of production, partly by direct expropriation, partly by the Enclosures Act, partly by the "inevitable" supercession of the small craftsman and artisan by large-scale industry.

Let us tabulate briefly the chief effects of the private appropriation of the instruments of production.

1. A man can to-day work in his native land, not like Adam, by going to the land and working, but by applying for permission to work to one of those men whose ancestors stole the land.

2. The working man is compelled to work on the owner's terms.

3. By the owner of any given concern, the worker must be regarded as a cost, just as a piece of machinery or plant is regarded as a cost.

4. Under a competitive system costs must be kept down.

5. The owner can only "afford" to pay out for his steel machinery so much as will pay for the oil and fuel to keep it just in running order.

6. The owner can only "afford" to pay out for his human machinery so much as will pay for the human oil (bread, butter and bacon) to keep the human machinery just in working order.

7. The human machinery or worker, in the aggregate, cannot buy up with the mere price of their human fuel, the whole of the product of home industry.

8. The owner *has* to market his goods somewhere, if he is to make his profit.

9. He cannot sell them at home because the low value of the fuel for human machinery has destroyed the home market.

10. He *must*, therefore, market them abroad. He is laid under the foreign-market necessity. He must be able to compel some foreign country to take his goods. The instruments of that compulsion are the fleet, the army and the air force.

11. Unfortunately, other industrial countries are simultaneously laid under the same foreign-market-necessity. Which country's owning class gets the market

depends on which country has the best fleet. This can usually only be decided by a trial of arms.

Once you allow the working population of any industrial mechanical country to be divorced from free access to the instruments of production (stage 1 in the above tabulation), then from that moment you have initiated a process whose inevitable end is war.

We need to start our pacifism where the war process starts (at stage 1) and not, with the League of Nations, merely at the point (stage 10) where the war process comes up to the surface and becomes glamorous with martial music; nor even, with the Social Creditors, (stage 6) at the point of distribution from the factory.

If we wish to *prevent* war we have to *pre*vent it—to get in before it has taken root. If we want to prevent war we have to liquidate those things which have made the instruments of production inaccessible to the population as a whole.

People are going short of things they want. And they needn't be going short of them. The effect of static political activity between 1900 and 1920 has been to cause a growing divergence between the obvious material potentialities and the evident miserable actualities. And in this gap between the actual and the potential as it stands there is enough gunpowder to blow up the world before it has had the inclination to bring the actualities to the potentialities.

The object of present-day politics therefore has to be to prevent too many people from realizing this divergence as an inward fact. Simultaneously, efforts, dictated by fear, are made to abolish this dangerous paradox of "poverty amid plenty" by abolishing the plenty, so as to get back to the good old days of "poverty amid poverty" when one could put the blame on nature. These attempts, systematized into a principle of government, make a fool of men's lives, as we have seen. But the fooling does not stop at that. *We*, through this system, stultify even Nature herself.

We make a fool of the land which draws payment for not growing hops or for not breeding pigs; we make a fool of the commons which are enclosed and the meadows which are cornered. We make a fool of the downs which are bought at a discount and sold, for a profit, into ugliness; applying to the land, the common heritage, the methods of the stock exchange and the white slave market. We make a fool of my garden which, in 1934, "unfortunately" had a magnificent crop of fruit. We make an abundance of apple-blossom a danger, and sunshine and lovely weather a menace to civilization. Loveliest of trees, the cherry now is discouraged from wearing too much white. The potato is fined for being too prolific. We say to the pear tree: "Go steady," and to the peach tree: "Careful, or you'll spoil the market."

Filthy insults! Monstrous indignities to inflict on the soil! And the ultimate irreverence of it all!

Heaven help the sanity of any visitor from Mars who drops in to the blasphemous twentieth century spectacle of Governments and statesmen and Ministers of Agriculture co-operating with frost and locusts and swine-fever and weevils to abolish the regrettable fecundity of the earth. Hand in hand with this inversion of Nature goes the inversion of Christianity; and from mere passive acquiescence in this condition of artificial scarcity we may yet see the Churches pass to offering up positive prayers for "Not *too* big a crop, O Lord." The world has become blasé about the miracle of increase, and the efforts of modern Scribes and Pharisees are devoted to trying to transform a fine catch of herrings into a few small fishes. It's a far call from Galilee to Grimsby.

Still, these attempts to abolish plenty, which now pass for contemporary "Politics," are bound to fail. Nature, like Mussolini's Italy, is prolific and intends to remain so. And the gap, between *what is* and *what might be*, remains also: in spite of all the restrictions and destructions. So, for politicians who have failed in this attempt to destroy the gap by destroying the plenty, the next best thing is to pretend that the gap isn't there. "We aren't really poor in the midst of plenty, are we. We are really poor in the midst of poverty." (This sort of remark, by the way, is nearly always made by someone who would quite obviously be rich in the midst of anything.) One way of pretending that the gap isn't really there at all is to treat it as an academic problem or a museum situation, something unreal and fantastic and quite irrelevant to the lives of ordinary people. Reference is therefore permitted in newspapers, speeches etc. to the paradox of "Poverty amid Plenty"; a phenomenon which cannot be visualized by a navvy, and which therefore means less than nothing to him. Who cares about wheat being used to fuel locomotives, anyhow? But to say that, although he's now working for 10½d. an hour, the navvy could easily be working for 1s. 10d. an hour, means something intimate to nearly everyone, and is therefore dangerous, particularly to the people who live in fear of plenty-potentialities. Hence "Poverty amidst Plenty" is a respectable subject for dissertation and polite regret; but to talk about a rise of 1s. an hour as being possible for every worker in the country is dangerously like sedition.

Finally, if it is found to be impossible to abolish the plenty safely and altogether, and if it is impossible also to prevent some people from thinking of the "paradox" as something faintly concerning themselves, then there's only one thing left to do. That is, to persuade people that really things are safer—and, therefore, to the bourgeois judgment, better—as they are. In effect, to put the Fear of Plenty into them. It may be true that we are only leading half-lives, but think of the dangers if everyone were allowed whole-lives! Better to hang on to what we've got, than go scrambling after some mythical Age of Plenty . . . With all its faults, there's a good deal to be said for leaving this old island to get along on its own . . . What was good enough for Great Uncle Augustus, etc. . . . This type of propaganda has the advantage of being simple; and it seldom fails in a crisis.

In all this, the plenty-abolitionists are wiser than they know. Dealing with devitalized people is really child's play. Man is a producing animal. A man in a job is inclined to be dynamic, and therefore dangerous. If too many people get producing, too many people get dynamic. That is the first danger. The second is that too much is produced, and what someone or other has called the "belly-grip" is relaxed.

It is a matter of fear-intuition for the present rulers to see that Unemployment rates should be low enough to ensure a supply of semi-blackleg labour waiting to step in. So that, if existing employees press for a full belly and the relaxation of the belly-grip, they may be discarded in favour of a gang of systematically devitalized individuals. This is not a piece of conscious malevolence; it is a policy motivated directly by fear.

The restriction scheme's belly-grip is maintained because if the working population suddenly had a full belly there's no saying what it might not do.

So with the spiritual belly-grip. Once relax the grip on the careful academic passwords, once let it be admitted that at least two ways have been found of bursting the world-scarcity inhibition, and no conscious person would stand for the incantations of seventy-five per cent of the existing rulers, dons and politicians.

The hops restriction scheme is designed to make the existent hop growers safe. No more people to grow hops. How awful to imagine that beer might become as cheap and plentiful as anyone wished! And just think of the terrible consequences, Auntie dear!

There is a hoop of steel round hops. There is a hoop of steel round the human spirit: an absolute restriction scheme to keep out anyone who might undermine the enthroned and established experts of the *status quo*.

And, as has been shown, this derives great support from executive statesmen and their lackeys, whose method of approach is to abolish the plenty if possible; failing that, to pretend it isn't there; and in the last resort, to persuade people that even if plenty is just round the corner, it is safer not to let it materialize. We might be worse off than we are.

We might be worse off than we are. That is the central idea of most conservative propaganda and political action to-day. The fact that this propaganda is successful suggests that a large number of people never stop to consider that in reality things could only with difficulty be worse than they are; or else that a large number of people are deliberately deceiving themselves. From the point of view of our permanent rulers there is always the danger that the entire nation might wake up one morning and ask itself fair and square over breakfast "Could we, in fact, be worse off than we are?" To which the fair and square answer might be "Conceivably we could be worse off. But it would take a tremendous amount of effort to make us so." In order to insure against this risk of sudden and widespread sanity, the authorities encourage us to take a daily newspaper. The point of the daily newspaper is to establish, as early in the day as possible, a renewed belief in the idea that we might very easily indeed be worse off; and that, moreover, if we try making changes or if we monkey about with the works in any way, we most emphatically *shall* be worse off, forthwith. The headlines tell us that there has been a hurricane in Florida, a judicial murder in Russia, a volcanic eruption in Japan, a pogrom in Germany and a riot in Paris. Thank God we're better off than that in our bright little, tight little island.

As a consequence, the newspaper-reading Englishman (whether he reads the *Express*, the *Herald* or the *Mail*) is, in fundamental sense, conservative. Political Conservative propaganda—(Record recovery from world depression: look how much better off we are than the Hottentots. It's true our kids have got measles, but the kids next door have got scarlet fever, thank God!)—follows on easily from all this and goes down without the consumer noticing the difference between diet and medicine.

There is another important influence working against the formation of an independent estimate of what politics ought to be about. That influence is the envy-emulation tendency inherent in the English "lower" and "middle" classes. Every Englishman loves a lord. Every Englishman feels that it might be rather fun if one could live like the Jones', or like the squire, or like Lord So-and-so or like Clark Gable. Probably this is a much more serious obstacle to a new order than any stock conservative propaganda—the small townsman's secret view of, or ambition for, himself. There are very few Englishmen of whatever way of life who can look through the *Tatler* without thinking that it might, after all, be rather fun to participate in the Claridges-Ascot routine.

But to each individual who dedicates himself to the

achievement of a new society there comes a moment when he rejects the idea of such a life-mode as an ambition-standard. Whether the "mass of people" can make this rejection before they have had a chance of experiencing the kind of life, is doubtful; but it is the crucial question. The rejection is easier for those who have seen the summit of an Ascot society, and have recognized its rottenness. The Oliver Baldwins of the world can hardly be under any illusion about the divine qualities of life at the top of the pyramid. Too many "socialist" supporters vote against the capitalist party not because they hate capitalism, but because they see themselves at the summit, instead of, as now, at the base, of capitalism. Because they see themselves as capitalists leading the champagne life, while, to complete the paradise, Lord So-and-so signs on at the Labour Exchange.

The small townsman, whose only recreation is likely to be the local cinema, sees himself as Clark Gable or Robert Montgomery in one of those Hollywood productions in which no-one seems to have less than a thousand a year, and whose life is shown to consist of an interminable series of cruises and cabarets. How, it may be asked, is the English small townsman going to reject the Clark Gable standard without spending a sufficient time in Hollywood? The chances are that he will want to assure himself of the emptiness of this apparent glamour, before he so much as considers a new society. Living at the base of the pyramid is acknowledged to be hell, but it is felt to be worthwhile to find out for oneself whether it isn't heavenly at the summit, before one considers trying a new sort of structure altogether.

In England the average villager still has some sort of admiration for the squire: sometimes even sees himself as squire. Even the occasional hatred of squire may spring from envy of squire's position. In Russia the summit of the pyramid was recognizable as being even more putrid than the base, although in a different way. The Russian aristocrats were palpably debauched and vicious and horrific. They were no peasant's wish-fulfilment. In Russia there *could* be a mass rejection of the aristocratic life as an ambition standard.

But the English squire is innately artful. He is bred to be adept at disguising, with a manner of cordial lordliness, the class structure and stratification of the village. Village cricket, the camaraderie of the hunting field, the visits of the squire's wife and the sack of coal at Christmas—these things are indispensable ingredients in the preservation of the English *status quo*.

There is one other thing which prevents the majority from forming a reasonable estimate of what politics ought to be about; and that is the difficulty of a man's judging what change is best for the world in general, apart from its probable effect on his own material position. The ideal state is seen by each individual through the refraction of his own present and future situation. When an elderly conservative laments that "we were all born forty years too late," he doesn't really mean that it would be better for the village children to be working twelve hours a day in the mines, as children were doing forty years ago. He just means that he, personally, feels that he would have been more comfortable if he had been born forty years earlier, when income tax was a shilling in the pound and there was only one Bolshie in the Commons etc. His own welfare becomes mysteriously identified with the welfare of everybody else. Hence the "we." On the whole, modern politics are not explicable in terms of plain self-interest. The kind of person who says "of course, I'm a conservative. I've got the hell of a lot to conserve" is now rare. The politics of any given individual person to-day are much more likely to be understandable if they are thought of as rationalizations of that person's own position. Even forty years ago it was genuinely possible (as well as convenient) for a landowner to believe that the feudal system was really in the best interests of the villagers; just as, previously, slave-owners had thought that slavery was in the highest interests of the slaves, and as, to-day, fox-hunting is claimed to be in the best interests of the fox. To-day, when the potentialities of machine production are becoming so perilously obvious, something subtler is needed. At this point in history therefore a way has to be provided whereby the poor can be richer without the rich becoming poorer. By the appropriate device the conscience of a sensitive land-owner or manufacturer can be soothed, and he can still feel that his own welfare is really very closely identified with the welfare of the people as a whole. No need to rob Peter to pay Paul. There is enough for everybody: it is only a question of tickets. How hard it is for a man who has much to lose (or much to gain for that matter) to make a just estimate of what sort of society will be in the best interests of the whole community.

A hundred and one things inhibit most people from making a reasonable judgment as to what politics ought to be about.

Is it possible for anyone to make such a judgment? It is possible to do something in that direction. For instance, it is possible to be aware of the influence of newspapers and the prevailing cultural climate, to discount the recommendations of one's own envy or sub-conscious grudges, to prevent, to some extent, one's own situation, and the way in which it is likely to be affected, from colouring one's whole idea of what is desirable for people in general.

Let's say that it is the business of politics to abolish the causes of the present armed neutrality between man and man, class and class, country and country. It is the business of politics to create conditions under which it may become possible for people to love their neighbour as themselves. Every man and woman in this country are, in some way, very much alike. But each man and each woman is, in his or her own way, quite unique. Until the needs which we have in common are satisfied, the things which are unique to each one of us will never come to the flowering. The immediate concern of politics to-day should therefore be to see that the world as a whole catches up with the material possibilities of living; so that, on a less cramped material basis, we may strive to create a society in which people, because they can be whole in themselves, can have a chance of being at one with each other.

How can these conditions be obtained? In my opinion there are at least two ways of doing it: of catching up with the material possibilities, that is, and of seeing that everyone inside the country is as little stinted as it is physically possible for them to be. Here's one way of doing it. I'm not sure that it's the better way, but, politically, it's more within the realm of probability than the other way. For practical purposes in England, what is desirable is limited by what it is possible to do; what ought to be done is governed by what can be done. No doubt what is desirable is that, overnight, everyone should come to the conclusion that it is in their true interests to work or perform a function rather than to own and be served. But in order to get on at all at this point we shall have to make the, at present, colossal assumption that, at the end of the next eight years, we shall have been permitted to retain a sufficient measure of Democracy to instal a veritable Socialist Government in the House of Commons. What next?

It would be convenient to start by finding out the nu..ber of people in the country. Call it forty-six millions in England, Wales and Scotland.

Secondly, it would be necessary to estimate how much food, clothing and shelter-material those forty-six millions would want to consume during the coming year. The making of this estimate should not present much difficulty; in fact a couple of willing statisticians could probably work it out in a week, with the help of the Co-operatives, the British Medical Association, the Board of Trade, etc.

Thirdly, compare the estimated total of consumption goods needed with the actual total of consumption goods for the present year. The actual total is certain to fall considerably behind the estimated total needed.

Fourthly, get out a scheme for increasing production up to the estimated desirable level of consumption, and use the idle plant and all previously "superfluous" labour for this purpose.

There is a lot of lee-way to make up and the chances are that, for the first few years, it would be convenient to utilize all your plant and all your labour for a full working week. When, through technological and inventive progress, the supply of labour becomes more than enough for the satisfaction of the real needs of the population, it will then be time to reduce the hours of labour all round.

The plan balances, consumption is always equated to production, because you can ensure effective demand by equating the total wages of the workers to the prices put upon the commodities which they have jointly produced. Such a rational system will not be attained overnight. It will, in present world conditions, only be achieved when the mass of people of this country are on the move.

In order to complete such a system, in order to ensure the maximum production desirable for consumption, it is necessary to transfer the industries of this country from private to public ownership, direction and control. That it is necessary to make the transference to public ownership would be questioned by many groups of people, including Social Creditors and Fascists. By Fascists, who give it as one of their professed beliefs that it is possible to plan for the benefit of ninety per cent of the population a system which is, *ex hypothosi*, a system run from the point of view of ten per cent of the population. By Social Creditors, who believe the same sort of thing; but who believe also that a Social Dole can be transformed into a Social Dividend simply by changing the name, without changing the underlying structural relationship. A "National Dividend" issued from an estate which is a privately owned and not a National estate, remains, in essence, a dole: something yielded grudgingly by the exclusive owners, and handed to the non-owners not because it is their right, but because the thing is no longer safe to withhold. The concession, of its nature, must be irksome to the exclusive owners, since it seeps away from them a jot or two of what they consider should totally belong to them; and, with this jot of ownership it takes away from them, as a class, a jot or two of their power over other people's lives. It loosens the "belly-grip." Their compensation lies in the fact that it may be expected to camouflage some of the disparity of income, to blur the divergence between the possibilities and the actualities of the majority, and, in general, to keep the excluded ones quiet for a bit longer.

On the other hand, it is premature for members of

the Labour Party to sneer at Social Creditors as being people who wish to let the world have it both ways; who want everyone to have their cake and eat it.

How does the Labour Party propose to transfer industry from private to public ownership? By expropriation? No, by compensation; by a full and equitable compensation. This seems to mean that though the influence of the shareholders, such as it is, will be removed from the direction and control of industry, they will still be secure in the proceeds of their bonds. (This of course depends on the terms of compensation, e.g., whether the compensation is to be paid from the shareholders' particular industry if the state of the industry "warrants" it, or whether compensation is to be paid out of the whole National Account. If the Labour Party is not meticulously careful about the terms of the compensation it proposes to allow, it will find itself accidentally administering a Corporative State.) Unless the Labour Party changes its mind when it draws up its next programme, the displaced owners will be amply secure in their compensation bonds. While they have the assurance of that amount of money, they will retain the power. To the extent of their incomes they will still be sovereign. Sovereign over their retainers and over the people whose livelihood must still depend on their gracious patronage. The even comparative "success" of the Labour Party's method will depend on whether they can evoke a sufficient increase in production, during the first two or three years, both to raise the standards of the workers *and* to pay the promised compensation. There is certainly a dilemma here; since to make compensation to the ex-shareholders a first charge on industry would be a pitiful betrayal of the Socialist idea, whereas, if compensation is not absolutely assured, and if, therefore, it is not made a first charge, then, it is argued, it will not be possible, in England, for a Socialist party to obtain an electoral majority at all.

The only proper method of transfer might well seem to be expropriation. The misappropriation has been going on long enough, in all conscience. A restoration of stolen goods is long overdue. But, in English politics, what ought to be done is limited by what can be done. The question is whether expropriation (with compensation only to prevent hardship) is a feasible proposition.

The answer, I think, is: "Not in normal times in England." Not, that is, until the excluded working-class are in a position to demand it, not until the workers are acclaimed as indispensable, not until its country needs them.

When, on the whole, does the country need the working-class? All of them. More, perhaps, of them than it can get?

The answer is: in war time. "Your country needs you." It's "thank you, Mr. Atkins," and so on. But in peace time their country doesn't need them.

And that is doubly unfortunate. Firstly, because it is a pity for everyone, and a hell for those who are not needed. Secondly, because until the working-class are needed, until they are indispensable, they cannot enforce this change.

The danger is that, if we try to procreate Socialism

99

before the conditions are ripe, we may produce some raging abortion.

I believe that, eventually, the only solution for the frustrations of people in this country will be Socialism; by which I don't mean State capitalism, or socialistic measures, or public utility companies, or metropolitan control of agriculture, or government from Whitehall, or Statishness in any form. I hate the State. But I believe in the majority—or I shall do when they come round from the social chloroform which has got them down and is now keeping them down.

It's difficult to believe much in the majority at present. Maybe this is one of the things which causes nearly every Socialist who happens to be politically active to ask himself at one time or another: "Is it worth it?" or, more impudently still: "Are they worth it?" It is this question that Sir Oswald Mosley eventually, and after a good deal of provocation, answered in the negative. "They" in the question may refer to the rank and file or to the leaders or to the "masses".

At some time or other one gets pretty exasperated with all three of these lots of people. Of the rank and file one can feel, with Mosley, as reported by John Strachey at Ashton-Under-Lyme: "This is the crowd which has prevented anything from being done in England since the war." Of the leaders "These, as custodians of democracy, behave inside the party like the flabbiest of dictators. These are not the men to do this thing." Of the "masses": "They are not worth it. They don't deserve it. They will not help themselves. They don't know what's good for them. We know what's good for them; and we shall give them as much as they deserve."

Probably this triple exasperation comes sooner or later to every Socialist who happens to be a member of the Labour Party. "Let them stew in their own juice." But, unfortunately for this superior attitude, they do not stew alone. You and I and all of us stew with them. Not one of us can get up and get on until everyone is in a position to get up and get on. Even if we, in our self-assumed superiority, decide to spend the rest of our lives giving the "masses" what is good for them, we shall be too busy holding the others down to get up and get on ourselves.

And, as the pace of history accelerates, there will be more of these catastrophes; to more and more people who are now, rightly or wrongly, in the Labour Movement, there will come the moment when the desire to interpret the half-articulate desires of most people is replaceable by a determination to see that most people get what they, the egregious ones, know is good for them.

A Socialism founded on a love for humanity in bulk may easily fail to survive this exasperation. A Socialism springing from an acquaintance with the minute particulars, from knowledge of individual people, from experience of some enslaved or frustrated particular neighbour, probably will survive.

It's easy to feel a Socialist in the village where I live; in the Tottenham Court Road it's equally easy for me at times to feel a Fascist. Almost every person in that village is a living argument for Socialism. Tom, with his troop of children, who was dead till Dick supplied him with beer-money which he could ill afford and brought him to life. Tom with his buoyancy and his potentialities which, at the age of forty, have only just begun to come out under the influence of a couple of pints, scratched for by a mate. Think what he might be if he didn't have to live his whole life on the margin of nothing-at-all. Dick with his eight children. Far too many children for a builder's labourer, as the visiting lady said. The working-classes simply bring it on themselves; they just won't exercise self-control. But she omitted to pick out the children she thought redundant. There are limits to shamelessness, even to the shamelessness of visiting ladies. Even she didn't dare to point to small Dick or young Tom and tell them that they ought not to have been born. Just: "Far too many children," she said, leaving it conveniently vague. I wonder what she'd have thought if she had seen young Tom go hiking off to the dairy as soon as her car was out of sight, to spend on a pint of milk the three coppers she had given him to spend on sweets.

Harry, who goes twenty-two miles to work every Monday morning, with his week's grub in a bag. They are no job for a married man, these vagrant electricity firms.

Jack, who might have been a more than average water-colour painter, if he hadn't had to spend twelve hours a day stoking a boiler.

Bill, a young jobbing gardener, and Annie, who's in service off and on. They've been walking out for nine years. They're badly frayed now; but still very much in love. And still sane.

The amazing thing is that the whole village is still sane. In all these people there is, however smothered, the image of God.

For me, the Tottenham Court Road is usually a different story. "I wish I loved the human race, I wish I loved its silly face." Certainly it taxes the imagination to see the image of God in the little padded-shouldered Jew and his painted woman walking along the Charing Cross Road. But, unless we are prepared to over-admit the divine potentialitities in these people (whom, incidentally we, through the way in which we allow things to be run, have assisted into ugliness) then the only attitude open to us is a mortifying cynicism, equivalent to death. You can say, if you like: "Nothing can redeem these people; they're too far gone." Possibly; but given a break and a level start, their children may have better luck. If you are not prepared to admit the potentialities latent in every single human being, then you have either to pack up, to abdicate from humanity altogether, or you have to think you know what's good for people and direct your efforts towards seeing that they get it.

If you admit the potentialities, then sooner or later you'll find yourself working for their release, for the breaking down of the frustrations which have laid hold on every one of us. I doubt whether you'll find any instrument of such a release other than Socialism. You will find no perfect instrument of Socialism in England. In my opinion the Labour Party is still the best bet;

though, in practice, the position of a fairly scrupulous socialist in the Labour Party is an embarrassing one. Either, as I think Middleton Murry has remarked, you have frequently to be dishonest with yourself in order to be loyal to Party policy; or else you embarrass your colleagues by blurting out something which you happen to believe, but which is not included in the Party Manifesto.

If you tend to get exasperated with the ungrateful masses you'll get twice as exasperated with the obtuse Labour Party, the Liberator presumptive of the masses. Perhaps the most common and fundamental exasperation springs from the fact that the Labour Movement is evidently incapable of making up its mind whether it represents a body of worms who are desirous of becoming birds, or whether it represents a body of worms who wish to change the whole basis of bird and worm society. The fact that it has not achieved either of these things is due to the inability of the Movement to recognize that it cannot achieve both of them.

Until the Labour Movement makes up its mind on this point the chances of its accomplishing anything at all are slight indeed. If it decides that it wishes to change the whole basis of bird and worm society it will have, as a preliminary, to do at least two important things for itself, before it starts in on other people. It will have to revise its ideas about leadership and it will have to learn something about British national psychology.

The Labour Party has a horror of dictatorships.

Personally, I believe that its instinct is right, though its conscious motives may be wrong. Unfortunately, however, the Labour Party tends to get Dictators mixed up with leaders. It doesn't want a dictator. It behaves often as if it doesn't want a leader. But it will have to have one. Not only the sort of leader that will help to get a sufficient majority in Parliament and in the country; but a leader of the kind that will be indispensable in the first two or three years of a Socialist regime—if it is to be a Socialist regime and not a Socialist Government. He will have to be totally disinterested, and a man of great moral infectiveness. Assuming that it is a practical, as well as an electoral, necessity for *some* compensation to be given to the expropriated, then production will have to be increased very considerably in this country in the first two or three years of office, if the majority of people are going to feel the results in their own material lives. The Socialist leader will have to be able to evoke and to reveal to people the moral, the religious side of this new kind of productive effort. If this cannot be done then the only possible hope lies on the far side of the hopelessness of another war.

Then there's the question of acqu intance with British psychology. I personally believe that Socialism implies a transcending of national boundaries, i.e., socialism is not consummate until it is a world socialism. But I believe also that the largest contribution which we, in Britain, can make to that world order, is to see that we establish here in this country a socialism which is genuinely appropriate to Britain. I believe that it is necessary to establish in Britain a British kind of socialism. (Hoots of derision from orthodox Marxists). I am quite sure that in order to get any kind of Socialism in Britain at all, it is necessary for political Socialists to have a much more just appreciation of distinctive British qualities than they have to-day. (It is for this, among other reasons, that I distrust the present permeation of the Labour Party by Jews.) A man is needed with the courage, clearsightedness and opportunism of Lenin, and with the astuteness, British-sense, intuition and controlled sentimentality of Mr. Baldwin (as he was up to the month after the 1935 election). Someone who will sort out the real from the spurious virtues of the governing class and give them their due.

Never has their ignorance of fundamental British characteristics served the Labour Party worse than in the debate in the Commons on the Hoare-Laval proposals. The national conscience had been violated in a distinctive and significant way. Hoare and Baldwin—the two people who had been responsible for the violation—were quick to recognize it. The Labour spokesman never grasped it at all. Their performance impressed the country as unfavourably as does a bowler who puts down the wicket when the batsman is "backing up" too far.

Supposing, however, that the Labour Party succeeds in putting its own house in order, what are the chances? Fair to very moderate. But that is not the main point. The main point is that, if we believe in our philosophy, we have got to go on fighting for it, chances or no chances. And to this end, it does no harm to have a

just appreciation of the difficulties. And the difficulties,
even assuming the existence of a Labour Party whose
leaders all wanted Socialism, are considerable.

There is the initial difficulty that, as Middleton
Murry has often pointed out "Socialism is not a great
moral issue in England." People ought to care about it,
one feels; but one knows they don't. It doesn't touch
them. You can't, on the whole, strike many sparks out
of the Great British Public at most times of the year by
preaching Socialism. You can rouse some of them at
times by preaching anti-capitalistism. But that is
hardly good enough. The English are at present
climatically non-Socialist, a fact which is utilized to
the full by Mr. Baldwin, who knows his England.

Too many of the people who are touched by Socialism
are long-haired and long ear-ringed and sit in circles
about Bloomsbury. Too many of the people who ought
to be touched by it are working for 10½d. an hour, or
watching football matches, or playing darts, or having
one more before ten o'clock, all the time.

There is another difficulty; the fact that, to our
rulers, democracy can only seem a permissible and
desirable thing so long as people don't use democratic
instruments for an assault on the central citadel of
our rulers themselves. When the mass of people seem
to be preparing to put through a democratic revolution,
the rulers naturally begin to wonder whether democracy is such a good thing after all. If there is one thing
certain it is that in ten years' time we shall no longer
have a capitalist democracy in this country. We may
have capitalism; or we may have democracy. It

depends on how many people prefer which of these two things, and on how powerful those people are, or can make themselves. At present, in England, the betting seems to be on capitalism and against democracy. Who can hope much of the results of government by the will of the people, when so many of the people themselves are too drugged, or bludgeoned or down-trodden to have any distinctive will of their own?

After all, it may easily be as risky a business nowadays to vote a "democratic" Government into power as to vote in a dictator. The check by the people on the subsequent activities of either Government is almost equally non-existent, in the present inert state of popular feeling.

Herr Hitler, before being just-voted into office, promised to nationalize the Big Trusts. Within a few weeks of coming into office he felt impelled to allow the Big Trusts to have the last word in governing the country. The people who elected him have no check on his actions. So far as one can see at present their criticisms will be confined to saying "Ja!" for the rest of their lives.

The Baldwin Government of 1935 came into office largely on its repeated pledges that it proposed to stand by the spirit of the Covenant of the League of Nations. Within four weeks of coming into office it had attempted to sell the League of Nations by means of the Paris "Peace Plan" and had committed an enduring blasphemy against the spirit of the Covenant. The people who elected this Government had no certain check on its actions. It's true that under a surprising and remarkable pressure it dropped this particular plan; but in a few weeks time it was getting at it in another way. A year later, Mr. Baldwin admitted in the House of Commons that it wouldn't have been wise to go openly to the country with a re-armament programme. A little deception of the electors was in the interests of their health. For five years—a period longer than the Great War—this Government can— unless something is done—continue to nod in West- minster. The criticisms of the electors fall on ears which are always capable of a safe and convenient deafness. In another four years time the early seed sown by the Government in Mukden and Paris will be coming to harvest in the shape of a critical European situation, and the phenomenon knows whimsically as "an appeal to the country" will be able to be carried out with as little risk of reversal as a Nazi plebiscite. *Fascisme blanche à l'Anglaise.* We laughed at the Germans when they voted 97 per cent solid for Hitler. But the Germans voted Nazi because they were afraid of being shot. The British, in 1931, voted National because they were afraid to think.

The truth is that Democracy is another of the things of which Capitalism has made a fool. There is another truth namely that to-day, England, or to be more accurate, we in England, are not ready for Socialism. In 1940 we might be ready for it. In January 1937 we are not. Admittedly this seems to mean that, for young men and women at present subjected to all the contemporary frustrations, there can—failing a widespread popular convulsion—be virtually no hope at all for another five years. But if, in 1935, we had had a Socialist majority of say fifty in Parliament, backed by a bare majority of electors in the country, and if that majority had tried to introduce Socialism (or if it had not tried to, for that matter) then for the young men and women aforesaid there would have been no hope at all for another twenty-five years or more.

Must we accept the implication that there is nothing to be done except to wait?

Socialism, we may agree, is impossible for four years at least. Even then, it will not drop from the skies. Socialism is not on the order of the day; but War may come to-morrow. Are we then helpless? Is there nothing that we can do from one election to the next? Does Democracy really consist in voting, once in five years, for one of three candidates whom one does not know? Can these Members of Parliament whom we chose, on the strength of certain promises to represent us—can they now do as they please with us, without check?

We sent them up to manage our affairs for us, to manage our foreign affairs in accordance with the principle of collective resistence to the Italian aggressor. They double-crossed us. And now they, the managers whom we appointed, are turning round and trying to rule us.

By damaging almost beyond repair our main instrument of peace, they have brought War closer to all our doors.

By their betrayal of the legitimate Spanish Government they have given a fatal testimonial to the efficiency of Fascist aggression.

Every day that these men remain in the saddle, the odds against peace grow longer.

Hoare went; swept out by a great wave of indignation. No single Party alone could have forced Hoare's resignation. It was the united hue and cry of Liberals, Socialists, Communists, Democratic Conservatives, people of no party who had been active in the cause of peace, and plain men whose sense of fair play had been outraged—it was this all-inclusive united pressure that got rid of the British Foreign Secretary.

Hoare went; but the men who approve his anti-democratic policy remain. From its behaviour to the Spanish people we can be sure that either the Government is in League with Fascism or else it is afraid of Fascism. In any case, it is a disaster for all those, of whatever party, who hope for peace.

Some all-inclusive united pressure must now be consciously mobilized to rid the world immediately of a British cabinet whose very existence in power is a standing encouragement to any Fascist who is thinking of committing an act of aggression. ·

Socialists, Liberals, Communists, democratic Conservatives and men of no party—we do not all agree about our long-distance objectives, nor about the pace at which alterations should be made. But we can all agree that, if any of us is going to have a chance of getting on with his own plans, peace must be preserved.

We can all go that bit of the way together. We can stand together to lessen the chance of war.

But there is another thing which must be preserved, if any of us are to get on at all. That thing is the right to work out our own agreements and disagreements among ourselves, in our own way. If we lose this right, we shall all be in the same boat. And we shall all be sunk.

We British tend to take our free speech and our rights as citizens for granted. But these rights did not drop from the skies. They were not a gift of God. They were struggled for by our fathers. If we do not uphold them by struggle, we shall lose them. The German and the Italian peoples have lost them. They no longer dare call their opinions their own. They are Hitler's men or Mussolini's men. They are not their own masters or their own men, any more. The rulers of Japan have gone one better. They have built "thought guidance clinics" for the people, where those suspected of "dangerous thoughts" are sent for treatment. And this *could* happen in England.

We take our rights of free association and Trade Unionism for granted. Yet they were won by struggle, and they were paid for with imprisonment and deportation.

The traditional British rights of free speech and free association are dear to British people of many political beliefs; people of many political beliefs must combine to uphold and extend them.

Millions of us, whatever our party labels, can move forward together towards an extension of personal and political liberty. Is there no economic advance which we can make together also? Personally, I believe that there is. I believe that the true Conservative is as keen as the Socialist and the Liberal on seeing that the scandal of having half our people undernourished and forced to live on a sub-human standard of feeding, is wiped out immediately. If the managers of the Zoo allowed their animals to be fed as badly as half our people are fed, they would probably be summoned for criminal negligence. I believe that millions of men and women, who hitherto have had no time for politics, would support a movement which was pledged to put an end to this state of affairs.

I am sure that at least twenty millions of British people would unite in demanding holidays with pay as a right for all. I am sure that they would unite in demanding a drastic shortening of the working life— shorter hours and pensions at an earlier age.

No question of surrendering principles is involved for those who support such a Front as I have advocated. I happen to have been for six years a member of the Labour Party, and to have fought the 1935 election as a Labour Candidate. I shall continue to work for the Labour Party and try to persuade people to join it. I believe that the greater the willingness shown by the Labour Party to take the lead in uniting the forces of progressive democracy in this Country, the greater will be the desire of ordinary people to join the Labour Party. But if some people are reluctant to join the Labour Party, I will not therefore refuse to co-operate with them on those objectives that we have in common —Peace and Freedom and economic advance.

There are twenty or twenty-five million people in the Country who can start to-day to go the next part of the way together. If we all refuse to go the next stage together, it is certain that we shall none of us survive to see the later part of the road.

How, then, can unity be created? Unity cannot be created.

I believe that, in the last half of 1936, a flow towards unity was becoming apparent. I believe that all one can do, all that needs to be done, is to remove the artificial barriers and obstructions which at present prevent people from uniting.

I believe that a passionate desire for peace and a loathing of mean and unworthy politics is naturally drawing together millions of British men and women, who are gradually learning not to be afraid of each other's party labels.

Two things are now standing between this desire for unity and its consummation.

The first is the question of an alternative Government. People who want to live in a pleasant house, don't burn down their bungalow before they've built the pleasant house. And people are chary of uniting to break up the National Government so long as they can see nothing very different to put in its place.

The second obstacle is that of the Party machines and the attitude of some of the party leaders.

It is significant that the leaders of the National Government have been quick to ridicule the idea of a People's Front. In due course, the leaders of the Labour Party have bestowed their official disapproval

on the idea. And the leaders of the National Government have not been slow to pat the Leaders of the
Labour Party on the back for their good sense in the
matter.

The fact is that not only the National Government
but also the leaders of the Labour Party may have
something to lose from the formation of a People's
Front. The National Government reflects the views of
certain powerful interests. Its Members of Parliament
are drawn largely from the ranks of retired army and
naval officers, and the families of shipowners, mine-
owners, bankers, financiers and big industrialists in
general. These people may be very admirable in their
own way, but their interests, owing to their very situation in life, must be widely different from, if not actually opposed to, the interests of ordinary men and
women.

Something of the sort is true also of some Trade
Union and Party leaders. They have a vested interest
in the positions of leadership—whether it's in the
matter of jobs, or prestige, or posts in the Cabinet.

Yet true leaders of the Trade Unions and of the
Labour Party need have nothing to fear. For it is
certain that once they give the lead to establish that
unity which is being groped for on all sides, their
prestige will be increased a hundred-fold.

On the other hand, if the leaders fail to lead their
followers, they will be forced, before long, to follow
them.

The National Government is trying to resist the
rising tide of progress. Some Progressive Party leaders

seem to be trying to resist the rising tide of unity. Both
have something to learn from King Canute.

The Chairman of the Labour Party, Dr. Dalton, has
recently said that if the menace of Fascism were to
become real inside England, the Labour Party would
have to reconsider its attitude towards a Popular Front.

If that is the case, then, in my opinion, the Labour
Party ought to have been reconsidering its attitude for
the last four years. Have we really got to wait until
civil war is in the air? Are we so certain that Fascism
will only come to Britain in some sort of fancy dress?
Isn't there a smack of a polite British brand of Fascism
in the growing process of the separation of ownership
from control exemplified by certain public corporations,
in the corporative efforts of Mr. Walter Elliot, in the
preliminary attack on the rights of the Trade Unions
and Co-operatives, in the elastic provisions of the
Incitement to Disaffection Act?

It seems to me that those of us who are in the Labour
Party have a fine, and a final, opportunity to give a
lead this year. If we don't take it, then we shall deserve
all we get—even if it's Mosley and his Black Beauties.

Once unity is established, power will not lag far
behind. Reactionaries of all ages have known this and
have struggled to prevent such unity.

So Bagehot, writing in *The English Constitution*:
"But in all cases it must be remembered that a political
combination of the lower classes as such and for their
own objects is an evil of the first magnitude, that a
permanent combination would make them supreme in
the country. So long as they are not taught to act

together there is a chance of this being averted by the wisdom and foresight of the higher classes."

National Government ministers know this too. Hence their applause when some Labour leader condemns a Popular Front.

For the fact is that whenever the people of Britain have stood together on a particular issue they have got what they wanted for themselves. In the past history of the British people lies the clue to their future.

In 1832, for instance, a vast stirring of the working-class and middle-class compelled the Government to extend the franchise, which had previously been limited to a privileged minority. In the middle of the century a similar movement compelled the Government to repeal the Corn Laws and thus lower the price of bread. Later on, by means of an epic agitation, the women of this country won themselves the right to vote. In 1935 the people of England forced the National Government to withdraw its Unemployment Assistance Board regulations. Just after the trick election of 1935 the hue and cry of all types and classes of people caused the resignation of a British Foreign Secretary. In October 1936 the people of London gave conclusive proof that Continental methods of provocation would not do in England.

The job in hand is now the mobilization of the power of twenty million British men and women for the removal of the present Government and for the placing in office of a true Government of the people.

"We are the people of England and we have not spoken yet."

Yet we, the majority, the eighty per cent of the population who do the jobs, have the best possible right to speak. The country couldn't go on without us. The remainder, the ten or twenty per cent, couldn't build a house by themselves, they couldn't drive a train or hew a lump of coal by themselves, they couldn't rear a cow or grow a cabbage by themselves. If they did succeed in growing it, they probably wouldn't be able to cook it by themselves.

We, who do the jobs, have the power. When we learn to act together, no-one will be able to resist our demands.

What shall we demand? What is it that we want in common? If we are going to have the greatest measure of agreement we don't want too many planks in our programme at the start. A six point programme for Liberal, Labour or Communist party candidates supporting a People's Front might read as follows:

1. Pacts of mutual assistance, open to all, to be concluded with France, U.S.S.R., and all democratic people's States, in the first instance.

2. Restoration of the rights of free opinion to public servants, of free association to Trade Unions and of free speech to everyone.

3. Work or full maintenance for all who are without jobs.

4. The means of adequate nourishment to be assured to all.

5. Pensions at fifty-five.

6. Holidays with pay and a drastic reduction of hours for all.

The fulfilment of such a programme would go some way towards lessening the anxiety and sense of insecurity under which people in this country are now living. For the middle-class worker at present most of the frustrations are non-material in origin. He usually has enough to eat; it is his mind and the rest of him which is unsatisfied. The man who works with his hands doesn't always even get enough to eat; for him the repair of the material situation has a primary urgency. But it is not merely a matter of substituting a set of well-fed navvies and farm labourers for a set of badly-fed ones. To them the fruit is the first necessity; but there are also the flowers to be considered, and there is, finally, the garden.

What will it mean to the man who works with his hands? Roughly it will mean that Tom, the cowman, will not have to stint his children of the elementary things, of milk, of eggs, of vegetables or of fruit. Fresh milk for tinned. English beef on Sunday instead of frozen. Butter for margarine. Cabbages, if not from his own garden then from next door, and not cabbages which have been kicked round Covent Garden. That Tom shall be able to provide his children with the elementary physical foundations, without allowing his wife to underfeed herself—as she will, given half a chance—and without forfeiting his Saturday beer-money. Particularly that there shall be no gap in Tom's living on a Thursday or Friday; but that one week's money shall last on to the next, and last comfortably, too. That there shall be some margin to his existence.

That for Tom and his wife three-quarters of their worrying shall become unnecessary; all the worrying about a rainy day, for instance, or the possibility of a torn muscle and no money coming in; all the worrying about having to quit at three weeks' notice, and the anxiety about the time when they'll both have done all the work that they've got in them. The elementary physical and mental things. A body not unnecessarily impoverished, and a mind not perpetually apprehensive.

It's not much to ask, in the twentieth century, in an age of plenty, in a Land of Hope and Glory, etc., etc. And it's not much to get. But it's a start; and people won't be in a position to become whole until they get it.

That is the first stage—fruit. Next—flowers—the individual and unbelievable blooming of Tom the cowman. And afterwards, at last, the garden; a joint and communal affair, in which, whatever the individuality and variety of the colours of the flowers, there is a harmony and a whole.

For the flowering it is necessary that Tom shall be able to have a life of his own. Time of his own, too. That he shan't have to work fifty-six hours a week while Dick, his eldest, is not allowed to work on the land at all, but has to go into town and be reduced from being a man to being one more name on the books of the Labour Exchange. (The final logical reduction, as we shall see, comes later when his name is transferred from the books of the Labour Exchange to the brass plate on the war memorial.) A room of his own, after he's had his tea, with some coal for the second fire, and books

and flowers and paint and writing things and a piano.
That, while Dick is not allowed to work at all, Tom
shan't have to stay back and milk on a Saturday when
he's wanting to be away in the next parish, going in
number eleven for the village side. That, while Dick is
forbidden to work at all, Tom shall not have to work
for fifty-one weeks in the year, and not be allowed to
take his family away to the sea for a good break; not
to Bournemouth or Margate necessarily either, but to
Cornwall, or Devon, or why not to Brittany or Madeira
or Naples? Sure it is that the National Government
will never arrange for him to do this. When the
National Government—a Government purporting to
represent every section of the nation—won the 1931
election, we are told that there was great rejoicing
among the hotel-keepers on the Riviera. Are we to
suppose that they expected to see every section of the
nation—including Tom and Dick—coming to spend
their holidays at Cannes or Nice? Or did they, unlike
the British voter, see that the word "National" was just
a new name for the old gang?

But when you've allowed Tom to flower a bit, and all
the other Toms, Dicks and Harrys to bloom a bit, then
the unbelievers will begin to gasp at the results. Because now it's as though we are living in a world which
has stopped dead at Winter; in a world whose Spring
is being systematically postponed. Of course, for the
folks who can afford coal and comforts and champagne
and dancing in the winter, it's not so bad, and one
gathers from the *Sketch* and the *Tatler* that they get
along nicely. But for the people, the majority, who for

their life and gladness, depend directly on the sun and the unrestricted bounty of the earth—for these people, this holding a shadow over the sun and this rationing of the earth is the very devil. And here we touch again on the root-nerve of the whole matter. The present arrangement: a subsidizing of the winter. The People's Front: an effort to let the spring break through.

Imagine what would happen if, in any one country-side, the seasons of the year got stuck at February. Imagine the turmoil and the frustration of the buds and the seeds. If the season wouldn't budge on at all, the results would be convulsive—riot and revolution in the soil and on the trees. But now supposing the season, from being held up in February, suddenly jumped on to late April. What a sprouting and a shooting and a singing there would be.

And when we stop subsidizing this false winter, and cease to stave off the sun and restrict the soil, when we let the larger Spring break through, and unchain the earth and the trees and the men, then what a singing and a wooing, what an outpouring of life there will be!

To lessen insecurity inside the national boundaries— that will be something. To be able to say: "Next week I'll take the wife to the pictures" or "Next summer we'll spend a week-end at Hayling Island," and to know for certain that next week won't see you stood off from your job, or that next summer won't see you genuinely seeking work—that will be something. It must be something in Russia now for the mass of the people not only to know where they stand to-day, but to have a pretty good idea of where they'll stand a week or a month or a year from to-day. In England now, you never can tell. It doesn't matter whether you're a casual labourer, or a craftsman, or a clerk or a man on the staff of a swank newspaper. They don't want to lose you but they just can't afford to keep you on. And there's an end of pictures and Hayling Island and plans in general. This, however, is a thing that we, in England, can put right, without reference to people in other countries.

But there's another thing. I often wonder whether those parents who go posting off from a christening to put their children down for Lords, and for the best public schools, ever count the odds? I don't mean the chances of Lords and the public schools being still in existence when the appropriate time comes; I mean the chances of their children being still in existence. Do they ever count the odds against the newly-born not walking into a gas cloud between now and then? Do they realise what is happening to the babies and children of Spain at this very moment? It's high time godfathers thought of giving silver gas-masks as christening presents, if they want to be realists, that is. And we're all realists now; we're all, except a few romantic scientists, learning our anti-gas drill. The crazy thing is that, simultaneously, we're all still making plans, taking out old-age endowment policies, and asking little Tommy what he's going to be when he's grown up. The answer, of course, is a hero.

I suppose that, in America, it's still possible to make plans, to forecast what one will be doing in 1953, and to reckon on a span of three score years and ten. But to-day in Europe

Who dwell under the shadow of a war
What can we do that matters?

What, as a matter of fact, can we do?

We can say "No." But it won't be much use saying "No" if, by consenting simultaneously to the production of war, which is a continuous event under this system, we act "Yes."

A League of Nations, many of which are imperialist states, must necessarily be a precarious instrument of peace. To the League as a whole falls the duty of stopping the war-process in its final stage, when it has gathered a momentum to which each individual state-member has, earlier, contributed. The League's present utility, in fact, lies not in establishing peace, in the full sense of that word, but in the postponement of a military conflict, which is itself the logical outcome of the way in which each individual League Member-state organizes its society at home.

If the League could postpone the military explosion for long enough to allow a preponderance of European countries to become socialist and thereby to withdraw their annual contribution to the causes of war, it would indeed have rendered a cardinal service. Whether it can do this depends on whether the State-members who are loyal to the Covenant can make sufficiently clear in advance their intention of countering each and every act of aggression by immediate, automatic and overpowering retaliation. This control of the world by the organization of fear is not an edifying procedure. But neither are the nations of the world edifying at the present time. A "peace" which owes its existence solely to the overpowering size and burliness of the police, instead of to the harmony and contentment of the public is, it may be conceded, no very great thing. But so long as we are unable to get the preconditions of that harmony established, so long, in my view, will bigger and burlier Police provide a better international chance for everyone.

Can the League of Nations even postpone the military explosion? Can it, from now on, make indisputably clear in advance its intentions to take immediate and overwhelming steps to counter each and every act of aggression? Can statesmen who still cling to the belief that the signing by their country's representatives of the Covenant of the League did not really in any way diminish their country's sovereignty—can such statesmen do any such thing? English opinion of all parties has been quick to condemn the dilatoriness and lack of obvious intention in France's attitude to the Italo-Abyssinian dispute; but who hopes or expects that England will anticipate, with a lucid clarification of policy, any attempt to alter by force the frontiers of central Europe?

While the large states in Europe and their Governments cling to the idea that their membership of the League of Nations involves no diminution of their sovereignty, the collective system for the restraint of an aggressor will only work successfully by accident: it will only be effective when its objective happens to be in line with the standing objectives of the main sovereign powers who are concerned with it.

The Policemen, though still brawny, are capricious. They only get on the track of a criminal when it suits them, and when the criminal seems likely to disturb their own personal quiet. But I am not convinced that even that is a reason for doing away with policemen altogether. It seems to me to be a reason for trying to obtain a better type of policeman and a police force not made up of burglars-on-holiday.

I myself have no doubt that England under a Government of the People could contribute the nucleus of a police force worth respecting. At any rate we should not have to endure the sight of our constables going about shamelessly flaunting the Versailles Old School Tie.

More important still, I believe that if the British People's Government were to conclude pacts of guarantee of mutual assistance in the first instance with France, the U.S.S.R., Czechoslovakia and the Scandinavian States, and were to make these pacts open to all to join in, it would give any potential Fascist aggressor something to think twice about. We must have an International People's Front within the League.

It has recently seemed at least possible that the Labour Party was going to choose its Armaments Policy as the particular weapon for its own suicide. The Party is certainly in a difficult, even impossible, position as regards this matter. It has advocated a policy of whole-hearted collective security, not excluding the use of military sanctions; but up till the Edinburgh Conference of 1936 it had refused to vote the armaments required for the sanctions, for fear that the National Government would use such armaments for other and quite improper purposes.

As the dictatorship countries become further advanced in their pregnancy of armaments, the Labour movement finds itself faced by the dilemma of *either* voting the National Government arms which it may proceed to use in alliance with Fascist states against Democratic countries *or* else of refusing to vote the Government arms and then, in four years time, after a hypothetical Labour victory, finding itself helpless before dictatorships whose armed pregnancy will have terminated, and who will by then be more than ready to deliver the goods.

I do not myself see what on earth the Labour Party, by itself, can do about this. But there is a great deal that an inclusive People's Front can do about it. A People's Front could encourage the Government to make this country formidable in arms, while at the same time making it clear that should the Government attempt to use those arms for an improper purpose, there would be an overwhelming upheaval in the country overnight.

Nationally, we are all frustrated by the bird and worm society which constrains us, internationally we are frustrated at every turn by that society's corollary of the sovereign state. Effectively, the supercession of the bird and worm society at home offers the best hope of destroying the conception of the sovereign state and the mess it makes abroad.

Once we get rid of the sovereign state and a number of national bird and worm societies, then, I am convinced the problems of raw materials and colonies and over-population will begin to solve themselves. In any case the problem of over-population and raw materials are only convenient economic pretexts for big chieftains who, having created a psychological unrest at home, are bent on making war anyhow, and who would be pained beyond enduring if other nations proved not only willing, but also able, to grant their demands. It is a fact that population problems of a sort do exist; but they cannot be solved by a successful war, though they may be eased by a sufficiently long and bloody unsuccessful one.

If it is true that, as Malthus would say, population is everywhere pressing against the means of subsistence, it is only so because the frame of the means of subsistence is, at present, an artificial one. What the population is pressing against, in my view, is the capitalist system in the national field, and the still-prevailing conception of the sovereign state in the international field.

At present there is a visible gap between the actualities and potentialities of production, between what is and what might be the condition of the world. It is in this lunatic gap that the so-called redundant part of the population is now eking out an uneasy existence. They are living precariously on the edge of the actualities, and are prevented or forbidden from helping to realize the potentialities. They are living on the margin of a world which does not apparently produce enough to support them, yet they are forbidden to proceed to produce more in order to support themselves. By the academic solicitude of leading articles in newspapers and by the careless pity of remote politicians, these marginal people are continually reminded that the world thinks them redundant, and that they ought never to have been born. Over five-sixths of the globe the querulous cry goes up "What on earth are we to do with the unemployed?" From one-sixth of the earth's surface the answer comes "Allow them to work." From the other five-sixths the only suggestion seems to be "Make them a first-class bonfire."

But it isn't only the unemployed who are in this fix, who are living in this gap. We are all, old and young, rich and poor, enduring the uneasy years of an interregnum. The old ways of life have become impossible; the basis of a new way of life is not yet available. All the partially compensatory elements of the old life have vanished. The old caressive relationship between landowner and "his people" has disappeared; and a new organic relationship between new people has not yet taken its place. The old houses are empty and unutilized; by the time that it will be possible to use them for schools or clubs or institutes they will probably have fallen down altogether. One half of the population lives its life in a state of reminiscence, looking back wistfully to the good old days of the past; the other half spends its life looking forward, but with a sinking heart, to the new days which are supposed to be coming in the future. No one dare contemplate for long the unspeakable present. And both halves of the population prolong their existence in a state of conscious or half-conscious fear.

But we cannot remain as we are. We shall have to make the jump forward into a new kind of world, or we shall have to watch the river of comparative liberty being turned abruptly back on its course. In ten years time either capitalism or democracy will have begun to make its final evacuation.

Within the next ten years, moreover, we shall have to release the true British national temper, we shall have to allow our traditional British characteristics to come to the flowering, or we shall have to witness the stream of British Nationalism being diverted and perverted into Fascism.

We are all of us suspended. We are all of us sunk in this space between two worlds. And unless we all make a unique effort, we shall none of us get out. With the prevailing nullity we can make no separate truce. And it's no use thinking that we shall be able to make the change on a great tide of hatred. It's no use crying out against owners and the governing class as though they were criminals. They are as much in the slime as the others; most of them are feeling as derelict in their way, quite as unhappy as anyone. Similarly it's no use yelling out against the armaments firms; they are no more specifically sinful than is the common hangman. They are caught up in a vast wheel of annihilation. It's true that it falls to them to put the finishing touches to the great prevailing death process. But it's the profit system, the whole property and profit system that is leading the world to its death. Outwardly, it is true that it seems to be doing this through its logical conclusion in the private profit in the manufacture of arms. But I doubt whether the metamorphosis of the arms industry from being a private capitalist concern to being a State capitalist concern would appreciably lessen the prospects of war. In either case the armaments industry would have an important bearing on a capitalist budget, a capitalist "favourable" balance of trade, and the provision of capitalist employment. The armaments industry is an integral organ of capitalism; from the general public it gets far too much of the credit for wars which it has only a very incidental share in pro-creating.

It is high time, indeed, to take sides. This, in effect, is a matter of life or death.

What shall *we* do?

To-day, in the opening months of 1937, the general situation is much as it was in the opening months of 1914. There is one difference. That is that the present situation is incomparably worse, in every possible way. Just as in 1914, the British Government to-day is neither inside nor outside the sphere of European conflict. War may come again in the next four months, as it came in 1914, because the aggressor nation will think that it can count on the neutrality of Britain. There is a second way in which the present situation is worse. The armaments race which led up to the

Great War for Civilization represented a yearly increase in the total armaments bill of all the Great Powers of only thirty-one million pounds. That was between 1908 and 1914. But between 1934 and 1935—the year which followed the wrecking by the British Government of the Disarmament Conference—the total armaments bill of the Great Powers went up by nine hundred million pounds. That is a process which cannot continue.

If we are going to have any respite from the insecurity which threatens us from inside and outside this country, we must have a new sort of Government in Britain. No single party can by itself turn out this Government in time. A united people's movement, a People's Front, can and must do so.

What shall *we* do?

If you are a Liberal, if you are a Socialist, or if you are a Conservative who believes that peace and freedom are more worth conserving than anything else, you can urge, inside your own party and in your own district the necessity of us all going the next part of the way together. All over England, in your own neighbourhood, the flow towards unity is gathering force. You, if you believe peace and freedom to be worth saving, can dedicate yourself to removing those obstacles which at present impede that flow, and to being, in yourself, a centre of unity and reconciliation. The alternative is to sit down and wait for the time when you are commanded to shoulder a rifle.

If you never had any time for politics, there are still things for you to do. Forms of the Popular Front are springing up all over the countryside and in London there is a central People's Front Propaganda Committee. There are songs to write, posters to paint, banners to sew, plays and films to produce.

The People's Front will not succeed on a great negative wave of hatred : it will sweep to triumph on a rising tide of religious fervour that will at last make this country of ours in truth a free, a merry England. British history will not come to an end when the preliminary programme of the People's Front has been fulfilled. Nor, on the other hand, even then will Socialism come over-night, or drop from the skies. But once we have achieved for ourselves certain economic advantages, such as a reduction of hours and holidays with pay, once the people are on the move and have felt their strength in action, then Socialism will no longer seem the remote and abstract thing which it now appears to so many.

The people will continue to make demands until all our fellow-countrymen are living up to the limit of the material possibilities which our country offers—until we have closed the gap between *what is* and *what might be.*

The People's Front is not a new party or political organization. Its advocates do not make promises to the people. Instead of saying "If you put us in, we will get you such and such a thing" they say "Can't you see that if all progressive parties and all progressive men and women stand together for the things which we have in common, that there is nothing we cannot get for ourselves? Can't you see, moreover, that, unless we stop quarrelling among ourselves, we are all of us sunk?"

For too long we have been appointing leaders to do something for us. Now before it is too late, let us do a thing or two for ourselves.

We believe that unity is necessary. Each one of us that believes this must himself become an agent of such unity. The Liberal has had some harsh things to say of the Socialist in his day, and the Socialist has had some pretty words for the Communist. We have no time now for such diversions.

On the People's Front platforms, also, unity is vital. It is perhaps the rarest thing on earth to find men, even of the same political faith, really and fundamentally supporting each other on a platform. But on the day when progressive men of different parties begin to support each other, both politically and personally, on the same platform, on that day the struggle against Fascism and reaction will be as good as won. This—this dynamic human unity for a common purpose on the part of men of different outlooks and beliefs—and the consequent transference of such unity from the platform to the audience—this is democracy's ultimate weapon against Fascism. This is the only answer to the carefully stage-managed demonstrations of Fascists everywhere, with their uniforms and their bands and their spotlights on the face of their single speaker—their Fuhrer, their Duce, their Leader, their brazen image—the symbol of a false Fascist unity, in which all the divergent elements have been, not reconciled, but hewn away.

Men, in fact, are instantly needed who, by their lives and their actions, will re-define the word comradeship.

It's easy enough to make the recommendation, more difficult to know what to do about it.

There is often too great a divergence between the way of life of, for instance, many Socialists and the ideals which they profess; and there is something more in this than a convenient handle for the *Daily Express*. To-day people, "Socialists" included, treat each other like muck. They may not do it intentionally; but they do it. Some might say that they can't help it, with things as they are at present. But no social revolution is worth a thought unless it enables and encourages people to treat each other more decently. And it is necessary that people who are going to bring about this sort of revolution should begin to treat each other and everyone else, more decently, now. That they should begin to close the gap, now.

A good many people treat other people like muck because they don't know them and because they are afraid to know them. A good many of the non-significant antagonisms between class and class spring from this cause. I myself have lived sufficiently near to both sides of the question not to believe much in the exclusive (or even particular) wickedness of the governing class or in the exclusive virtue of the working class. In actualities I believe that they are both equally petty, and equally bourgeois, too, for that matter; in potentialities, about equally spacious.

Do I mean that I want a society like some enormous

Oxford Group, embracing Madam and her butler on equal terms? I do not.

Do I mean that I want to see the navvy and the squire going arm in arm into the public bar? Not necessarily; though no doubt they'd both learn something, would both come out fuller men.

I do mean that if, by a social revolution, we hope eventually to establish something which we are pleased to call a "classless Society," then someone, some body of people have got to become classless before that revolution, if a majority of people are going to have a chance of becoming classless after it. You can't make a new world without new men.

How, are you going to do it, is the obvious question, to which, unfortunately or fortunately, I have no answer to make. The journey, or the turn, into classlessness, is a journey which one makes alone. It is a private affair. It cannot be induced, though in theory it can facilitated.

Earlier in this essay we have been scoffing at our present rulers for being afraid of the consequences of the release of plenty, for being afraid of the repercussions of a life which is completely new. In this orgy of derision we have overlooked the fact that we, too, are afraid. We must be. If we weren't afraid, things would have begun to happen already. "The secret of liberty is courage."

At bottom, it is a matter of putting off the old man and putting on the new man. It may take time—generations. It may take only the break, the vision of a moment. It may come through the trial of a new way of life, ratified by the conviction of an instant.

However long it takes, it will be worth while. And the present keeping afloat in, and contributing to, a world that has had its day, is not worth while.

For the moment, all that one can say is that many people who have rallied to the idea of a People's Front have themselves found new life in joining in this general struggle for the rights of the people.

The world, and people in general, must have something to do. Either they must make life or they must make death. Under the present circumstances, in all countries of the world with the exception of one, preference is given to the making of death. At present making death gives more employment; it also pays better. And so, because we can think of no other way, we give each other employment by preparing to kill each other. In due course, we set about killing each other. Who said the capitalist system couldn't solve the unemployment problem? "Unemployed! Back to the land!" Man, in this age of abundance, cannot live by bread alone, so he is forced to live by drawing a wage by making shells and bombs which, in the fullness of time, may be used to extinguish himself, his wife and his children. (As a shareholder of Vickers recently observed: "This is a business, not a philanthropic institution."). In the old days, Christians had to live by making textile machinery in Oldham, by means of which, eventually, the Japanese could starve their mates in Preston. To-day, Christians have to live by making gas masks through which their

137

infants will die slowly from gas manufactured by their mates for sale C.O.D. to the Christian enemy. Never can the human family have been bound together by such indissoluble ties.

> *"We are not divided*
> *All one body we*
> *One in truth and Doctrine*
> *One in Charity."*

On a village green in England, there stands a gun. On one side of the gun there is a plate with an inscription showing that it was made, in 1913, by an English firm. On the other side, there is another plate, on which is inscribed the legend: "Captured from the Germans, the Hundred Days, 1918." There it stands, the final symbol of the motto of capitalism: Profits at any price. Profits at *any* price.

I finished writing this article on November 11th 1936. Down in Sussex, where the two minutes silence did not have to be hewn out of the solid noise of twentieth century civilization, one had leisure to reflect on this momentary truce. Even in Barrow, one supposed, there was a truce for these two minutes—during which the men in the armament firms rested from the making of shells for the next war, and thought of the Germans and the Englishmen who had been killed by similar shells in the last war.

There was a truce over parts of England. But in Jarrow and South Wales and Tyneside there was no truce from hunger and anxiety and despair. There was no truce in Spain, where black troops and German and Italian aeroplanes were making Spain a land fit for Spaniards to live in. There was no truce in Ethiopia, where the Fascists mercenaries were bringing civilization and gas to the people of the Western Abyssinia.

There was a truce in parts of England. But elsewhere the killing was going on. The sharp thrust of the bayonet, the careful agony of poison gas, the slow wastage of starvation.

And from now on, in the war against poverty and murder, against tyranny and anxiety and despair there can be no truce, until this struggle is won.

On the evening of Armistice Day, back in London again, I went to a cinema where they had a film of that morning's ceremony at the Cenotaph. We were shown pictures of the King laying his wreath, of the massed bands, of the crowd which packed Whitehall, and finally of the faces of the ministers in the Cabinet. Then spoke the Commentator: "Let us hope that our statesmen will see to it that the events of 1914 to 1918 are never repeated again." Looking at the faces of these "statesmen," Baldwin, Simon, Chamberlain, Attlee, MacDonald—helpless, shuffling, bewildered figures—I thought I saw why it was that Governments, all Governments of whatever colour, were always too late. Too late on Abyssinia, too late on Spain, too late in dealing with the claims of the German people, too late perhaps on the second World War.

And to-day, in November 1936, when the history of 1914 is on the point of repeating itself, it seems so frightfully important that, for once, we should be in time.

It is within the power of ordinary English people and particularly of men and women of the English countryside, to be in time and to put an end to these things. These each have their village war memorial. The names on its brass plate were once men who worked and lived with them. The gaps left by their going are not filled as they are in a town. The waters do not close above them so easily. By casual incidents, one is constantly being reminded of how good Tom was at darts, of the Irish song which Dick always sang on the Club-night before Christmas, of how no-one would dare to sit in that corner of the bar if Harry were here to-day. It took a good deal of money to reduce each of those men into a name on a brass plate—five thousand pounds, to be exact. And of that money, two thousand five hundred pounds went into the tills of arms' firms.

One does not know how many of these lives were extinguished by shells or guns made in England by their cousins. Dick, who died to make the world safe for Democracy in the Dardenelles, was almost certainly put out by one of the products of "a business, not a philanthropic institution."

And, unless we stop making death now, the village might just as well put up a memorial to-day with the names of all the inhabitants inscribed on it, and then, when business—as opposed to philanthropy—ripens to its final stage, put a tick against each name as it duly pay; its dividend. Obediently, we get up in the morning, and go along to work, to make our little quota of death, so that our children, on their twenty-

first birthday, shall have something coming to them.
The alternative, of course, is to begin making life.

Life will come. The thing which remains in doubt
is whether it will come before, or after, at least one more
world war. And that, gentle reader, is a matter for
you to decide.

III

THE POETIC APPROACH TO REALITY

J. S. COLLIS

THE POETIC APPROACH TO REALITY

I

I SAT at the edge of the last crag on the farthest cliff before the ocean in the west. I looked down upon the rocks round which a crowd of seagulls wheeled like snowflakes falling. I looked across at the green territory, the liquid waste, the heaving fields, the range upon range of water hills that led to a new world. I looked up into the extravagant and erring clouds that sailed with summer in their flight and winter in their mien. I looked back over the treeless eternity of bog, and watched the sun go behind a mountain made gloomier by that glow.

At one point in the cliffs there was a cleft which led to a little harbour with a tiny pier. Rows of flat-bottomed boats lined the shore behind. I walked down to that sequestered bay, and as I arrived I saw a procession of men and youths approach, led by two priests. They reached the boats and the quayside. The people devoutly gathered round the priests who then *blessed the bay*. After that ceremony about half a dozen of the curraghs were launched and manned, and from the pier the priests blessed the crews and sprinkled holy water upon them. Then there was a grand race. And by this time many others besides the crews turned up and watched the spectacle. Girls looked on, and old women with shawls over their heads sat like boulders on the hill above, watching their sons and their son's sons taking part in the ancient rite.

It was a pleasant and moving spectacle, I reflected, this manner of inaugurating the mackerel fishing season. It seemed a fitting ritual. It was an *act of reality*. It had its root in meaning. Here on a far shore of the Atlantic Ocean superstition came into line with the profundities of mystic worship. That act was crude. That act was primitive. But it was a salutation to Powers beyond the understanding. At the root of religion is Awe. At one end of the scale, for the primitive, it is dread; at the other end, for the mystic, it is love. Only the middle stage is accursed. The intellectualist—fixing his gaze upon mental pictures of chaotic atoms—alone is cut off from communion.

Must these Irishmen here, I wondered, as I gazed upon their finely individual faces, pass into that middle stage? By the law of movement, under the Sentence of this Era, must they descend into that valley and drink of that cup?

II

THAT scene recurs to me again. For most people
who read books are in that middle stage. They
cannot go back; and they do not know how to go forward. They have got stuck. Most of modern civilization is jammed with excess of itself—like the London
traffic.

Having learnt how to exist with such remarkable
mechanical efficiency, we have now to rediscover how
to live creatively. That may not be impossible.

Very likely our first task is to think straight. That
calls for no special brain power: only for something
rarer and more simple. It involves the capacity to
reason from a central experience.

Let us hold on to that last sentence throughout.

Not long ago I travelled to America on the *Majestic*,
a ship which takes only five days to get there. It was
winter, and one night there was such a furious storm
that the great liner could not move forward at all and
had to stop. But on the morrow hardly any of the
passengers knew that there had been any special storm
or that the boat had stopped. No-one was afraid of the
ocean; few even observed its presence. No-one was
afraid: and at the same time no-one had any reverence
or faith. Now, supposing they had been able to *see*
Nature instead of merely regarding her as a conquest of

Man; supposing those ocean walls, those raging peaks and Alpine valleys, those Mont Blancs of wave, had frightened them a little—would it not have been a fruitful experience? Would they not have been awed by the wonder of the almighty hand? Would they not have felt that such a kingdom of glory and power was in itself a sure and certain sign of everlasting purpose? Would they not have drawn nearer to the Mystery of God, and trusted that that which could and did thus govern this could govern all with final justice?

It may seem strange that without Fear there is no Faith; that to restore faith we must restore fear. But it is not hard to grasp the paradox that the fearing are finally faithful while the unawed remain for ever sceptic. In the Middle Ages three monks came to Father Sisoes and complained that they were continually pursued by the terror of three things: fear of the river of fire, of the worm which dies not, and of the outer darkness. When the saint made no reply they were greatly depressed. Finally he said: "My brothers, I envy you. As long as such thoughts live in your souls it will be impossible for you to commit a sin." I am not intending to hark back to the ancient Christian ascetic piety as it survived in the Oriental Churches when the priests advocated that believers should *cultivate fear* as the only road to salvation—(especially fear of the Day of Judgment). I do not approach the subject on that plane. But on a purely *naturalistic* plane I am ready to insist that Vision unfolds from the womb of fear.

But to return to the travellers on the *Majestic*, before they could have drawn closer to the Mystery in the way I have outlined above, they must first have had that much *experience*. Those thoughts would be the fruit of what they had felt—as all true thought is. But to-day people actually think before they feel! Instead of experiencing and reacting to the universe they literally sit down and puzzle over it in the abstract.

III

EARLY MAN was in a different case. His capacity to experience was in excess of his capacity to think straight. He felt the presence of the *numinous* too much and too often. He felt himself hedged round by the divine or the devilish on every side. To him it seemed that the sun, the moon, the stones, the rain, the trees, the corn, were each and all presided over by a separate god who would not disdain to receive adoration and sacrifice. He believed that there must be vast companies of gods because manifestations of their skill were so numerous; "for it was impossible to believe that the splinterer of the crag was also the shaper and guardian of the hyacinth. Having reached this conclusion, he poured from his brain a multitude of deities: he associated the groves with fauns, the woods with dryads, the water-lilies with naiads, of whom even so late in the story of mankind as Ovid's day there were one hundred in the River Anio."[1] The fact that these gods remained permanently invisible did not matter, for nothing is more remarkable than how little the mind inquires about such things when the emotional need is otherwise. The Greeks are held up to us by our schoolmasters as being highly intelligent; nevertheless they experienced no intellectual discomfort in believing in a

[1] "Solitude" by Norman Gale (Batsford)

150

whole hierarchy of Gods dwelling on Olympus, often visiting the mortals below and sometimes even marrying or violating them—but never once can any Greek have seen one of these gods in the flesh walking through the street.

With the advance of Science and its investigations, its new material knowledge, and verifiable evidence another frame of mind was created. The sun was discovered to be, not a god, but a ball of incandescent gas. That finished it. It was labelled and explained. No-one need take any further notice of it—while a sun-*worshipper* was obviously as mad as a naked man. Then, while rivers of description (mistaken for explanation) were poured out concerning everything until the thing itself, the Real, the Actual, was submerged, the same scientific forces began to build up machine civilizations which removed men ever farther from the necessity of living in contact with elementals. Water: fire: air: earth : of these the air alone was used in the customary manner. A tap for the water, a switch for the fire, and asphalt over the earth, made short work of their actuality, their magic, and their awefulness, until at last the time came when to *soil your hands* was used as a term of reproach.

Once the whole of England was rural. There is a certain amount of it still left. But eight-tenths of the people prefer to live away from it in towns—not in sensible cities but in barbarous and extraordinary places which have no connexion with the earth at all. The result is that hardly any of the people are in touch with the rhythm of life and able to apprehend that it has a meaning. Hence Meaning is thought and argued about instead of being felt. Under such conditions the simplicities of religion vanish and the life of the nation becomes horribly lacking in spirituality. A climate of thought congenial to men who prefer to think and read instead of looking at the phenomena of life, envelops them, while the scientists pretend that investigation leads to revelation! In this atmosphere religion is submerged, and the religious sense of unity between men, classes, and nations no longer exists. The thinking is as sterile as the feeling is impoverished. The vision of life becomes so narrow that the mind is forced to try and satisfy itself with theories of progress and evolution.

It is strange that during this middle stage we should pride ourselves upon our sensibility. We only mean intellectual refinement. As I write, the Chinese Exhibition is open. Everyone knows that the most remarkable phenomenon exhibited there is the pottery. But before we can really appreciate it, certainly before we can feel it, we have to be highly intellectual *connoisseurs*—and even then we cannot react to it with the same immediacy as unsophisticated, primitive people. Some Burmese peasants dug up some pots and brought them to my eldest brother who guessed that they must be of great value. The peasants were highly excited with their find before my brother made it known that it was valuable. "How did you know that they were antique?" he asked, "as you can have no experience in dating porcelains." "*We felt the power*," they replied. Frequently when they find an old porcelain they feel power given to them over their neighbours, or they see apparitions, or receive the power to heal the sick. So immediate is their contact.

I am not here advocating (even if it were possible) a state of mind, a sensibility so keen, that we are thrown off our balance at the sight of a pot—though I am free to say that such a state of quivering *aliveness* might well seem an enviable condition even to the corpses sitting in the Athenaeum or in purchasing articles at Woolworth's. I am drawing attention to our present state when our capacity to feel either fear or wonder is meagre. I am not holding up the primitives for imitation; they often attempted to placate their Gods in a mann'ʼ that was scarcely more attractive than that employed by the nineteenth century industrialists who offered up a generation of children to the machines in Lancashire. Their feeling was good but their thinking was bad.

IV

THERE is a third stage which can be reached, when thought again becomes linked with feeling, and knowledge with experience. This is a much more satisfactory stage than the first or the second, for the thinking is worthy of the feeling.

Again we stand confronted by the phenomena of Nature. Again we stand on the shore. This time we pronounce no judgment—in terms of the ocean being good or bad. We imagine no gods. We stand observing that *it is*: there are only five profounder words in the language—the words which Jehovah used to describe Himself—I AM That I Am. Before we really see that It Is we may have to stand there for some time, even years perhaps; but at last we do become seers and receive the revelation.

Once we have learnt to do this, to gaze upon one of the outstanding phenomena of Nature, we cannot help reaching out towards sanity. We cannot help it; for once we have learnt to see, then our questions and doubts become less intense. We are so intrigued with the *spectacle* that we become far more concerned with praising it than with the problem of how it got there or why it was made at all.

We gaze upon any single thing: ocean, or foxglove, or maggot, that spotlessly clean little creature into which dead flesh turns, that miracle in whose ceaseless chase is mirrored the principle of everlasting action and the merciful remorseless turning of the Wheel! We look upon them until we do see that each is perfect, until we do know that God, wherever and however conditioned, can be trusted. There never was a more spontaneous or happier expression of that insight than when Browning cried out so gladly: "God's in His Heaven; all's right with the world!" Some people have regarded that exclamation as if it were a solemn and risky theological assertion. Browning did not mind at all *where* God was, whether in Heaven or in some other geographical area, or in some area that knows not geography; but he was quite sure that things were ultimately all right.

We gaze upon these things, we gaze upon the pure phenomena—and we feel awe and love. This condition is attended by one strikingly pleasant fact: namely, that science can never undermine it. For while in that condition we are greater than scientists, we are seers. We welcome the scientific analysis of the daffodil but we know that it cannot tell us so much about the flower and its significance as a poem on it by Wordsworth.

Thus do we attend at the death of gods. We no longer feel the necessity to create gods—nor heavens nor hells. Nor do we any longer puzzle over the problem of God the Father of all. We have disposed of many things. But one thing remains—the everlasting, the continually reborn impulse to worship the Mystery. That remains. That is a fact as flinty and as well supported by verifiable evidence as any of the rocky

facts of science. The gods with all their paraphernalia
and property are dead by act of science. The Acts of
the Scientists have been necessary in the history of our
liberation. With one gesture they have swept away the
inessentials. The conceptions vanish and the core of
religion once more is seen.

It will be observed that the requirements for reaching
this third stage are not intellectual ones—though to
understand why that is so calls for an intelligence often
found lacking amongst the intelligentsia. In this third
stage it is seen that the only thing to do is to abandon
argument and investigation as a means of arriving at
Truth, and to rediscover the actual phenomena of life.
Those who adopt this device are often called Mystics.
They are *content* with sensing the Mystery. They are
not mysterious people. They do not see visions: they
develop Vision. They do not possess second sight—
whatever that may be. They possess first sight. They
are practical poets whose prerogative it is to uncover
the veil of illusion that comes between us and reality.
They are often spoken of as possessing a higher state of
consciousness than their fellows. It would be simpler to
say that they are men who have taken the trouble to
keep awake, to be *fully* conscious. They join hands with
the primitives. But they are in a more satisfactory
position: for with them dread has been turned into
Awe, and wonder into Love.

V

I WOULD like to try and put this into a few concrete images. Three men stand upon the soil: a primitive, a scientist, and a man in what we are calling the third stage. The primitive, seeing the corn rise, hearing the thunder roll, is wonderingly afraid and thinks it expedient to pray for the blessing of the permitting gods. The scientist sweeps aside all such nonsense and investigates the phenomena showing that a stone isn't really a stone, nor weight weight, nor speed speed, nor anything really what it appears to be. He is so successful that he begins to give the impression that the universe is somewhat of a chaos and not to be trusted—that it is in fact a purposeless flux. The third man regards the same phenomena. Perhaps the best way to study his approach will be to take a definite historic person in this stage of consciousness—Walt Whitman, for instance. He does a practical thing—he writes a poem. And the poem he writes is *This Compost*. I will quote it in full, and I will venture to ask the reader to read it, as I do myself, sentence by sentence, in no hurry, and with no attention paid to its form.

THIS COMPOST[1]

I

Something startles me where I thought I was safest;
I withdraw from the still woods I loved;
I will not go now on the pastures to walk;
I will not strip the clothes from my body to meet my lover the sea;
I will not touch my flesh to the earth, as to other flesh, to renew me.

2

O how can the ground not sicken?
How can you be alive, you growths of spring?
How can you furnish health, you blood of herbs, roots, orchards, grain?
Are they not continually putting distempered corpses within you?
Is not every continent worked over and over with sour dead?

Where have you disposed of their carcasses?
Those drunkards and gluttons of so many generations;
Where have you drawn off all the foul liquid and meat?
I do not see any of it upon you to-day—or perhaps I am deceived;
I will run a furrow with my plough—I will press my spade through the sod, and turn it up underneath;
I am sure I shall expose some of the foul meat.

[1]"Leaves of Grass," Cassell.

3

Behold this compost! behold it well!
Perhaps every mite has once formed part of a sick person—
*   Yet behold!*
The grass covers the prairies,
The bean bursts noiselessly through the mould in the garden,
The delicate spear of the onion pierces upward,
The apple-buds cluster together on the apple branches,
The resurrection of the wheat appears with pale visage out of
*   its graves,*
The tinge awakes over the willow-tree and the mulberry-
*   tree,*
The he-birds carol mornings and evenings, while the she-birds
*   sit on their nests,*
The young of poultry break through the hatched eggs,
The new-born of animals appear, the calf is dropped from the
*   cow, the colt from the mare,*
Out of its little hill faithfully rise the potato's dark-green
*   leaves,*
Out of its hill rises the yellow maize-stalk;
The summer growth is innocent and disdainful above all those
*   strata of sour dead.*

What chemistry!
That the winds are really not infectious,
That this is no cheat, this transparent green-wash of the sea,
*   which is so amorous after me,*
That it is safe to allow it to lick my naked body all over with
*   its tongues,*

That it will not endanger me with the fevers that have deposited
  themselves in it.
That all is clean forever and forever,
That the cool drink from the well tastes so good,
That blackberries are so flavorous and juicy,
That the fruits of the apple-orchard, and the orange-orchard—
  that melons, grapes, peaches, plums, will none of them
  poison me,
That when I recline on the grass I do not catch any disease,
Though probably every spear of grass rises out of what was
  once a catching disease.

4

Now I am terrified at the Earth! It is that calm and patient,
It grows such sweet things out of such corruptions,
It turns harmless and stainless on its axis, with such endless
  successions of diseased corpses,
It distils such exquisite winds out of such infused fetor,
It renews with such unwitting looks its prodigal, annual,
  sumptuous crops,
It gives such divine materials to men, and accepts such leavings
  from them at last.

I wish the reader was by my side. For I would like
to see what effect those words had on him, if any. To
reside in this third stage does not call for a scholastic
equipment; but it does demand a faculty which not
everyone possesses. The *a priori* capacity to wonder
must be there: you must be able to behold that compost
and behold it well. There are some who could not. But

those who can really take in that chemistry may be "terrified at the earth" in a manner that would seem ridiculous to the average chemist, but they will also possess a faith and a perspective equally foreign to him.

VI

THIS approach to the matter though not intellectual in the sense that it relies upon accumulated
data, nevertheless requires a more complete exercise
of Reason than that offered by the man who, using only
his brain, forgets to use his eyes and his common sense.
Those who are fond of employing the words "verifiable
evidence" in a tone of voice which seems to imply that
they have a monopoly there, should be invited to
remember that it is precisely verifiable evidence and
striking scientific proof which is celebrated in Whitman's poem.

But owing to the residence of our schoolmasters,
professors, and theologians in the second stage of consciousness, such an approach is not encouraged. So
proud is the intellect, so strong its armament, so cunning
in its capacity to keep up its dignified position. The
atmosphere, the climate of thought in which we move
is against a man reading *This Compost* and in favour of
his reading, shall we say, *The Purpose of God* by W. R.
Mathews, Dean of St. Paul's. Both the poem and the
book are about the same thing. They both witness to
the existence of Cosmic goodness, purpose, and guidance, on the basis of what has been well called "The
Argument from Design."[1] Walt Whitman is content

[1] See "Farewell to Argument," (chapter iv) by J. S. Collis (Cassell).

to invite the reader to behold the earth and to behold it well; and having done so to go away a faithful man —and to *remain* faithful to what he has felt! Hard, very hard—and possible. But the theologian makes no such declaration of independence. He says in effect—"Such an experience of beauty and miracle is admirable, and is certainly one of the chief causes of belief in God. But before it can be taken seriously it must be shown to be coherent with the rest of human knowledge and with the scientific view of the universe." That would serve as a typical remark of those who dwell in the merciless marshes of intellectualism. It is like saying—"You can't have religion until you have subscribed to the Times Book Club and got out and mugged up all the appropriate books on the subject and thus seen how everything really does fall into line and support your experience." Such an exhortation will scarcely help the man or woman in the street. How could they find time for this? Yet the solemn schoolmasters of the world will offer degrees and prizes to the student who takes such advice while regarding the reader of *This Compost* with good-natured insolence. And conventional youth (that is *all* youth) will acquiesce and will pile its shelves ever higher with books of information and discussion believing that if only it can read enough and take the matter far enough Truth will be reached. The happy fact is unacknowledged that to investigate is not to reveal and to describe is not to explain. There is no Answer to the riddle of the world. There is only a Sign. We call it Beauty. That is what Keats meant by saying that Beauty was

163

Truth and Truth Beauty and that that recognition was the foundation of creative philosophy and of creative living.

To men like Keats the signals of Beauty, the promise contained therein, overcome all other considerations, they "obliterate" as he said himself "all consideration." To the author of books such as "*The Purpose of God*" they can do no such thing. Experience is not really regarded as so important as rationalization. But let us not forget that Keats is here the *natural* man; we can all follow his method and see what happens. And what happens is that we become more alive—which is itself a sufficient justification for the method. We are enabled to begin to live and to think creatively and even enjoy ourselves. We no longer think and feel and experience all in water-tight compartments. What happens to us during the day is not considered as one thing and our profound speculations concerning the universe as another unrelated thing. What we call æsthetic experience is not regarded as something to be enjoyed on Tuesday afternoon and forgotten on Thursday when we speculate on the problem of evil.

There is a flower called the bluebell. I have read a good many books, but I think that I have got more out of the bluebell than out of almost any book. I have been unconscious of how much it was advancing me. I used to leave London for the day and seek out various bluebell woods in Kent. Those hours were very creative—though unconsciously so. I used to sit down and pluck one bluebell and gaze at it closely for some time, examining the minute detail of its inexhaustible beauty, and I remember saying to myself more than once—"This is enough to go on with." I was unaware then that I meant the same as Whitman when he said: "All truths wait in all things"; the same as Wordsworth when he said "To me the meanest flower that blows can give thoughts that do often lie too deep for tears"; the same as Blake when he said that we should learn "To see a World in a grain of sand. And Heaven in a wild flower. Hold Infinity in the palm of your hand, And Eternity in an hour." Increasingly from that time I have felt that this and this and this Particular holds by its own sheer existence enough to justify the Universe. Such experiences give me my philosophical starting point, my basis, my authorities, my witnesses, my faith. First comes the experience then the thought. But we must not let any professor label it as "poetic experience" or something. Never let us label it, but make use of it, get the fact into our heads (oh yes, we need the mind very badly, we need to use Reason) that such experiences do not lead to salvation but *are* salvation—and are at the mercy of no scientist or theologian.

VII

THUS we are engaged in an Activity. We have undertaken a line of action which results in Vision. We can see at last—that is all. But how different is the station of one who can see from one who cannot. For *until the eye can see the mind demands its concepts.* If we cannot see we must compensate ourselves with theories —which, alas, may be disproved. It is useless to make faith parasitic upon some intellectual concept or hypothesis that can be challenged. Let it rest, let it be parasitic upon what we experience in a bluebell wood. On that basis we are safe, and indeed, saved. We are no longer in the miserable position of the man whose theory may have to be scrapped. "If your old religion broke down yesterday" says Undershaft to Major Barbara, "get a newer and better one to-morrow." But what is the good of that if it also is in danger of being scrapped? There is no *variety* of religion: there is only a variety of religious experience— that need never be scrapped. One of these varieties is æsthetic joy such as we have been describing. I am emphasising it here because as the centuries advance it becomes the chief variety, the norm. In the early days men were never content with the experience, they insisted upon saying, not that they had seen such and such a signal of Truth, of All's Well, but that they had seen a god or gods, and promptly invented names for them. That was all right for the inventors, but unfortunately their followers took these symbols as the chief thing and never bothered about the experience which begot them. But the experience is everything, otherwise the symbols are hollow. In the past, men could not see this and loaded themselves with these chains believing them to be garlands. And there is still a company of men called theologians who discuss and compare these chains and fail to realize that the experience that gave them birth is the only thing worth discussing.

This method then, is an Activity. Something is done, a position is taken up, a beginning is made, *a central experience feeds the mind.* Why do so few attempt it? I think I know why. They refuse to try it because it doesn't appear to solve the Problem of Evil. And they feel that they can't make any headway until it is solved.

But the man wishing to enter the third stage, makes a list of things that don't matter. He heads this list with four items: problem of evil, free will, whereabouts of the Creator, and immortality.

He does not imply that they do not concern him. But he sees that for the moment they are simply obstacles to advance, and that so long as he remains puzzling over them he will get nowhere. And he scents the possibility that if he advances in experience the problems may change or fade—especially if dropping the argumentative mode, he exercises his faculty of acceptance. Professor Gilbert Murray when suggesting that Euripides in *The Bacchae* was reaching

167   12

out to a conception of the Kingdom of Heaven being within you here and now, not to be obscured by striving and hating, goes on to say "On one side this is a very practical and lowly doctrine of contentment, the doctrine of making things better by liking and helping them. On the other side it is an appeal to the almost mystical faith of the poet or artist who dwells in all of us. Probably most people have had the momentary experience—it may come to one on the Swiss mountains, on Surrey Commons, in crowded streets, on the tops of omnibuses, inside London houses—of being as it seems, surrounded by an incomprehensible and almost intolerable vastness of beauty and delight and interest—if only we could grasp it and enter into it!"[1]

Even if we do not grasp it or enter into it, we have done well; and if we choose to understand it creatively we will have done better than if we had read the latest Survey or Intelligent Guide. As far as the attainment of Vision is the aim, one such intimation, presage, apprehension, inkling, glimmering, surmise, intuition, if made part of our life and of our knowledge, is worth all the book-knowledge we can store up.

---

[1] "The Athenian Drama," vol. iii. (Allen & Unwin.)

VIII

WE may then begin to find that the Problem of Evil shows signs of yielding—though not to a rational explanation. The best illustration of this irrational conquest may be found in one of the earliest plays ever written—and one of the best. It needs cutting down and tightening up, but even so it is a remarkable drama. The technique belongs to Bernard Shaw, though the conception of the play could never enter the Shavian mind. In the Book of Job we find a great deal of what we are accustomed to imagine as modern discussion of the problem of evil—for in all ages it is generally discussed in much the same way, and if it has yielded to solution it has always been the same solution (there cannot be two).

You remember the story.[1] Job was a man of substance with large estates and happy family. All went well with him, and he himself did nothing wrong. Suddenly his good fortune came to an end. One day when at dinner, four messengers in succession arrived to tell him that his oxen, his asses, and his servants in one place; his sheep and servants in another place; his camels and his servants in another place; his sons and his daughters in another place—had all been destroyed.

[1] With acknowledgments to the "*Aryan Path*" for allowing me to reprint this study of "Job".

Job was overcome and rent his mantle and threw himself on the ground. Yet still he worshipped God, crying out immortally: "The Lord gave and the Lord hath taken away; blessed be the name of the Lord!"

But there was more to come. Satan, from going to and fro on the earth, and from walking up and down in it, had observed that while a good man will bear the loss of property and children with fortitude and piety, he will not, however good he is, submit without protest to a disfigured body and ill-health. "Touch his bone and his flesh" Satan says to God: "and he will curse thee to thy face." And God decided to test him in this also.

In consequence Job finds himself covered with boils from foot to head. He takes a trowel to try and scrape them off, and sits down among the ashes. This is too much for his wife who says to him: "Curse God and die." But Job still stands firm. "What?" he asks, "shall we receive good at the hands of God, and shall we not receive evil?"

Hearing of his calamities his friends come to see him. At first they are so shattered at the sight of him that they are dumb and sit down with him on the ground without speaking for seven days and seven nights.

They then make up for this silence. Job himself leads off by breaking into imprecations and cursing the day he was born in an almost Celtic stream of poetic fury: "Let them curse it that curse the day, who are ready to raise up their mourning. Let the stars of the twilight thereof be dark; let it look for light, but have none; neither let it see the dawning of the day!"

At the spectacle of his casting down Job's friends are alarmed and try to find reasons to justify the situation. Eliphaz the Temanite, Bildad the Shuhite, and Zophar the Naamathite are intellectualists and moralists. At not inconsiderable length they make out a case for God, and by insisting that Job has been guilty of sins and hypocrisies, endeavour to show how his sufferings at the hands of God may be reasonably accounted for. But they fail to convince even themselves. The sincerity of Job's replies disarms them: for not only does he maintain his innocence but even in his pain and perplexity he refuses to deny his feeling of the Divine Wisdom. Though he has said to corruption: "Thou art my father:" and to the worm, "Thou art my mother and my sister," though all have turned away from him in abhorrence, he nevertheless suddenly bursts out: "Oh that my words were now written! Oh that they were printed in a book! That they were graven with an iron pen and lead in the rock for ever! For I know that my redeemer liveth, and that he shall stand at the latter day upon the earth." And to his tormenting friends he turns and says: "But ye should say, Why persecute we him, seeing that the root of the matter is found in him?"

When Job and his friends have exhausted themselves with argument, a young knowledgeable fellow called Elihu the son of Barachel the Buzite bursts out and is under the impression that his special pleading for God is highly effective. But suddenly God Himself appears in person and punctures him by saying: "Who is this that darkeneth counsel by words without knowledge?"

And at this point the drama reaches the high moment we have been awaiting when a solution to the mystery will be offered.

We know what to expect. We have been prepared for an authoritative statement from God himself reproving Job for complaining and pointing out that God has ends in view not to be comprehended by mortals, or that He has been testing the good and pure man, or other plausible and rational explanations (though always exposed to a further why?). But God does not do this. He doesn't mention Job's situation at all! Instead he points to the magnificence of creation. He witnesses to the sublimity of His works. He rehearses the glory of life. "Knowest thou the ordinances of heaven?" He cries to Job: "Canst thou bind the sweet influences of Pleiades, or loose the bands of Orion? Canst thou bring forth Maxxaroth in his season? or canst thou guide Arcturus with his sons? Canst thou lift up thy voice to the clouds, that abundance of water may cover thee?" He shows the strength of His government and the dominion of His command over all things as over the ocean to which He saith: "Hitherto shalt thou come, but no further: and here shall thy proud waves be stayed." In a series of flaming poetic images He summons up the incomprehensible miraculousness of creation before Job's inward eye, and then reminds him of the existence of the wild goats and hinds, of the wild ass, the unicorn, the peacock, the stork, the ostrich, the horse, the hawk, the eagle, the hippopotamus, and the crocodile.

Job is overcome. He does not submit—he *accepts.*

Suddenly he accepts and cries out to God: "I have heard of thee by the hearing of the ear; but *now* mine eyes have seen Thee. Wherefore I abhor myself and repent in dust and ashes." He has suddenly become a seer and his mind is set at rest.

But why? What revelation has he received that he has not had before? What new argument has he heard? Has he not reasoned along those lines himself, or tried to? Did not Elihu the son of Barachel the Buzite advance much the same view?

No. The answer is No to all those questions. He has suddenly left Rationalism behind—and reaches another viewpoint. God has not spoken to him rationally. He has not given him a new argument. He has given him a new perspective. He does not even try to convince Job in the manner in which Whitman approaches the problem in *This Compost*. He does not point to Purpose or Design. There is no teleological persuasiveness whatsoever in the Almighty's discourse. He mentions animals that offer the feeblest support for that kind of approach. He speaks of the ostrich which leaves her eggs in the dust "and forgetteth that the foot may crush them, or that the wild beast? may break them. She is hardened against her young ones, as though they were not hers, her labour is in vain without fear; because God hath deprived her of wisdom, neither hath he imparted to her understanding." Nor does the hippopotamus with its unseemly gait and its bones that "are as strong as brass" provide in its person the best possible example of a perfectly designed universe—yet the Lord is careful to say that this creature no less than

173

the monstrous crocodile and the eagle whose young ones suck up blood, is "the chief of the ways of God." His method is not to convince by reason but to convince by the *power of mysteriousness.* The tormented soul of the sufferer is appeased, not by the sudden light of a good reason, but by a sudden feeling of *an intrinsic value* in what appears to be the very negation of reasonableness: the incomprehensible becomes, in itself, fascinating, and more inspiring than the comprehensible: the thought descends, the thought occurs, that All is Well, not because there are reasons for that thought but because there are no reasons. And the passage put into the mouth of God by the great dramatist does indeed "express in masterly fashion the downright stupendousness, the well-nigh dæmonic and wholly incomprehensible character of the eternal creative power; how, incalculable and 'wholly other,' it mocks at all conceiving, but can yet stir the mind to its depths, fascinate and overbrim the heart."

That profound German scholar and brilliant writer, Rudolf Otto, from whose "Idea of the Holy"[1] I have just quoted, mentions the story called "Berufs-Tragik" by Max Eyth in which the theme in *Job* finds a modern setting. It tells of the building of the mighty bridge over the estuary of the Ennobucht.

"The most profound and thorough labour of the intellect, the most assiduous and devoted professional toil, had gone to the construction of the great edifice, making it in all its significance and purposefulness a marvel of human achievement. In spite of endless

[1]Oxford University Press

difficulties and gigantic obstacles, the bridge is at length finished, and stands defying wind and waves. Then there comes a raging cyclone, and building and builder are swept into the deep. Utter meaninglessness seems to triumph over richest significance, blind destiny seems to stride on its way over prostrate virtue and merit. The narrator tells how he visits the scene of the tragedy and returns again.

"'When we got to the end of the bridge, there was hardly a breathe of wind; high above, the sky showed blue-green, and with an eerie brightness. Behind us, like a great open grave, lay the Ennobucht. The Lord of life and death hovered over the waters in silent majesty. We felt His presence, as one feels one's own hand. And the old man and I knelt down before the open grave and before Him.'

"Why did they kneel? Why did they feel constrained to do so? One does not kneel before a cyclone or the blind forces of Nature, nor even before Omnipotence merely as such. But one does kneel before the wholly uncomprehended Mystery, revealed yet unrevealed, and one's soul is stilled by feeling the way of its working, and therein its justification."

It is a very suggestive passage. The greatness of Man no less than the mystery of his life is witnessed to. Nature cannot triumph over the superior man—even sheer negation cannot annihilate him mentally. Nothing in Nature would seem more negative than a plague of locusts, for instance. Yet that living cloud of consuming destructiveness and meaningless wrath, that waste of life o'erthrown, that rain of flesh and blood, is in itself so colossal an event that it overwhelms the mind and passes out of the range of comprehension, but not really and not *finally*, we feel, out of the range of Meaning.

IX

THIS unrational approach may not seem wholly satisfactory or within everyone's reach. That is true. But it is more satisfactory and more within our reach than the intellectual approach, which, remember, after centuries of acutest speculation has brought us no peace. That alone should be sufficient to condemn the method to death. But it dies hard. People still feel that Free Will, for instance, can be investigated intellectually by scientists. It can. But to what end?

This is brought out rather well in Sir Arthur Eddington's "New Pathways in Science."[1] Let me say at once that with Eddington we are *not* in the presence of an excellent scientist who, while knowing what constitutes an atom, does not know what constitutes religion. Quite the contrary. Eddington, Einstein, and Whitehead, it is comforting to reflect, possess the true religious vision—they are men, that is, who acknowledge that religion is founded in Awe, and that so long as we are capable of Awe we are safe (often called saved). Eddington devotes a short chapter disposing of Bertrand Russell's ill-informed representation of Eddington's position. It is a necessary and welcome reply, for in "The Scientific Outlook"[2] Russell makes the following remark: "Sir

[1] Cambridge University Press
[2] Allen & Unwin

Arthur Eddington deduces religion from the fact that atoms do not obey the laws of mathematics. Sir James Jeans deduces it from the fact that they do." To which Eddington makes the admirable retort: "Russell here attributes to me a view of the basis of religion which I have strongly opposed whenever I have touched on the subject. I gather from what preceded this passage that Russell is really referring to my views on free will, which he appears to regard as equivalent to religion."

Eddington is clear in his mind that to possess religion, or at any rate its foundation, you need not have solved the problem of free will. Nevertheless he has much to say regarding Determinism; for please note the following unhappy circumstance—which I will venture to emphasize by giving it a special paragraph:

Namely, that whereas the fundamental nature of religion can be stated in a few words, discussions on the circumference, such as the tantalizing one of free will, can take up pages and pages, thus giving the impression that religion itself is somehow of less importance, and obscuring the fact that these problems will fall into place if we suffer the invasion of religion.

Eddington gives much space to Determinism on the ground that there is a certain importance in attempting to show how the idea of free will is now compatible with physics. But here I pause again before the strangeness of the human mind. There seems to be no Absolute in the minds of those who contemplate the big questions. In the history of thought we find that the idea which delights one man will distress another. To one person our descent from Eve is the thought which gives him most pleasure, to another it is our ascent from the ape. To one man the idea that God is *above* provides the maximum of stimulation, to another that He is *within*. One will bank everything upon environment forming character, another on character coming first. And so it is with Determinism. Russell, while missing one point, hits another in saying that Eddington is pleased with the idea that atoms occasionally hop unlawfully, while Jeans is pleased because he thinks they hop lawfully. And in "New Pathways in Science" we find Eddington defending himself against Sir Herbert Samuel who, banking everything on the idea of causality, has declared that Eddington is robbing the public of its most cherished beliefs.

What I am proposing here is that we cannot reasonably hope to make headway towards knowledge of the Will within ourselves by objectively investigating the hopping of an atom. That is a grave statement to make, I know. If accepted it would involve an unheard of amount of silence. But let us not be bamboozled by the heavyweight volumes on the subject. Their authors hold that whether we are or are not in a position to hear the voice of God can only be decided by examining the physical world.

I remain bold enough to doubt it.

It would seem that Eddington also doubts it. He writes: "A theory of matter has to correspond to our perceptions of matter, so a theory of the human spirit has to correspond to our inner perception of our spiritual nature. And to me it seems that responsibility is one of the fundamental facts of our nature. If I can

be deluded over such a matter of immediate knowledge—the very nature of the being that I myself am—
it is hard to see where any trustworthy beginning of
knowledge is to be found."

It would be hard to find a stronger or clearer or less
compromising statement than that. A child could
understand it: and yet it says everything—certainly far
more than learned volumes on the subject. It says that
our feeling of responsibility, of inner compulsion
(however feeble), provides the only approach to an
answer concerning the question of free will or the Voice
of God. It may not be a completely satisfactory answer,
nor a thorough-going solution. We have a strange way
of assuming that all problems are solvable: that if we
only go on long enough we will find the solution, as to
a cross-word puzzle: but that is pure hypothesis, there
is no guarantee that all problems are solvable. It is
extremely unlikely that we will ever get any nearer to a
solution of the determinism problem than our sense of
responsibility. And that ought to satisfy us. After all
we are human beings—not merely intellects. And we
will have a far better chance of living creatively if we
try and accept that responsibility instead of exhausting
our vitality in discussing whether we really have the
power to do so.

X

THE third and fourth problems which were relegated to a subordinate place by our student entering the third stage were—the position and condition of God, and the question of Immortality. I think we must agree that the question where exactly God is and what He is, is one with which we can make no progress. Luckily it is not important. Our experience of the divine is all that matters. If we are lacking that experience then only will we feel the need to erect theories concerning God's nature—there can hardly be two opinions on that vital point, that pleasant, peace-bestowing point. And as regards Immortality, we must acknowledge that our beliefs concerning that problem must essentially be intellectual, we can have no experience of it. Therefore in this essay I do not feel entitled to say anything about it, for you will scarcely be willing to tolerate speculation from me when I am advocating experience-knowledge. . . . And yet I would modify the above to this extent: certain experiences do perhaps point to something in the nature of *re-incarnation* as extremely likely. I am beginning to come round to that. But I hope it is not true. For it is a conception which gives me no pleasure.

XI

NOW where have we got to? Let us gather the thread of this discourse before proceeding. My main point has been that in order to free our minds from lumber, to think creatively and thereby live creatively, we should rest our philosophy, our religion, upon those experiences when we have, however feebly, felt an *assurance* of the Ultimate Righteousness. It is not an uncommon experience; but it is uncommon for people to *understand* the matter properly and make use of the experience—yes, I must repeat that the mind has heaps to do, we need our minds urgently in getting this matter straight, in creatively understanding our intuitions. But once we have got it into our heads that we have at any given time had a most important experience, then we have already gone a long way. And the ground is cleared for further advance. It does not matter what the experience is so long as we recognize it as the real thing. Nature will be the best medium for some, love for others (why should love, the most thrilling of all experiences, be excluded from philosophical significance and kept in a queer water-tight compartment?) while for a few there will be reserved such an experience as Job had. But once the matter is rightly understood the ground is cleared for more such experiences all of which now add to our philosophy and enrich our religion, instead of being cut off as being too pleasant or not solemn enough to be taken seriously.

That's our starting point. Once we have a footing by reaching the root of the thing and have freed ourselves from the conceptual substitutes for religion, we can begin to move. And we become intellectual again. I mean that once we have *accepted* the universe, willingly, then intellectual explanations do become helpful. A close examination, for instance, throwing light upon the necessity of pain as coincident with joy, becomes a consolation once we have made that acceptance. That willing surrender—not unwilling submission—must be made first, otherwise the explanations provide no stimulus: for the reply can always be made: "I see your point; the world would not be able to exist at all unless there was a balance of opposites. Quite so. But I happen to think it a great pity that it should exist at all if it can only do so under those conditions." There is no answer to that. The man who, quite legitimately, utters it, will have to remain in that position until he has had some such experience as we have been talking about. No-one can answer him or pull him out. For though you can hand a man knowledge, you cannot hand him experience. But once we have accepted the universe then we can really delight in examining its mechanism, and with advantage to ourselves and to all mankind become scientists and investigators.

Take two remarks from Chekov.[1] On two different planes. The second no good without the first—or any

[1] "Notebooks" Gorky, (Hogarth Press).

13

way unable to make any great appeal by itself. The first belongs to what I have called the third stage.

"Essentially all this is crude and meaningless, and romantic love appears as meaningless as an avalanche which involuntarily rolls down a mountain and over-whelms people. But when one listens to music, all this is—that some people lie in their graves and sleep, and that one woman is alive and, grey-headed, is now sitting in a box in the theatre, and seems quiet and majestic; and the avalanche is no longer meaningless since in nature everything has a meaning. And every-thing is forgiven, and it would be strange not to for-give."

That is the utterance of pure experience—with music as the stimulus. He could say no more than that. He could mount no higher. The last sentence carries us to the exalted place.

In the same tiny and wonderful Notebook Chekov entered the following:

"So long as a man likes the splashing of a fish, he is a poet; but when he knows that the splashing is nothing but the chase of the weak by the strong, he is a thinker; but when he does not understand what sense there is in the chase, or what use in the equili-brium which results from destruction, he is becoming silly and dull as he was when a child. And the more he knows and thinks the sillier he becomes."

Those delightful words do not belong to the same plane as the preceding ones, but they could not have been uttered save by a man in the third stage, and they really can only be appreciated by those who can appreciate the first ones. But provided we do reach that plane of acceptance then we can welcome the marriage of heaven and hell upon the basis of which the world is run. Our adjustment to the facts of life becomes healthy, so that we see vitality and innocence where formerly we might only have seen "Nature red in tooth and claw"; and our adjustment to our own individual psychologies changes, for we perceive the creative possibilities in the conflictions of which we are made up, we do not lament the tension in which we live (if that is our nature), knowing how much of the music of life is played upon the tightest strings. The law of compensation, the law of the necessity of opposites, the laws of conflict, as taught by Blake, Emerson, Carpenter, Keyserling, Havelock Ellis and other moderns should be followed up as intellectually as possible. For (provided we have a goal) knowledge of the necessity of polarity both in the world and in ourselves, *reconciles us to our destinies.* There is forgiveness, even self-forgiveness, for weakness and folly and sin.

XII

I HAVE just employed the phrase—our adjustment to the facts of life. A philosophy of vital, creative living, not to say some slight possibility of happiness, lies concealed in those words.

Many people still think that there is nothing so important as the acquisition of facts. As I have said before, it is the predominant notion to-day that the more facts we know the better. Take the following passage from Sir Arthur Eddington: "It would be as difficult to select a typical star as it is to select a typical animal to represent the animal kingdom. But the sun is about as typical as any. It is not at all extreme in any of its characteristics; and around us there are numerous stars that are practically replicas of the sun. The sun is 33,000 times greater than the earth in mass, and 13,000,000 times greater in volume. Its diameter is 865,000 miles and its mass is 2,000 quadrillion (2.8027) tons. Its mean density is rather greater than that of water." One is amazed. Not at the information given so much as at the power of man to give such information. It sounds as if the scientist had been there and counted it; but the fact that he does it through an instrument of his own making is a still more miraculous circumstance. Yet only a very unbalanced view of education will emphasize the importance of such facts. For everything now depends upon the *attitude of mind* which we bestow upon established facts. Facts in themselves are not shocking, stimulating, or depressing. The depth of the ocean, the height of the mountain, the heat of the sun, exist as facts: but our attitude towards them is determined by ourselves. They are terrible or splendid according to the health of our vision. The super-scientific, the super-reasonable question to ask is: Can we so cultivate our vision as to see the phenomena in terms of aweful beauty rather than of mental perplexity? We know that we can, and that such a science is of more importance than any other to-day. There have never been too many such scientists. There may never be.

Few realize how much power we possess in this field. In us dwells the kingdom of heaven. In us dwells the kingdom of hell. In us dwell purity and impurity, good and evil. We bestow what significance we choose upon the facts of life, we transform them, we shape them like clay according to ourselves. All the facts of all the world, all life—we shape. In daily life also, and all the time; the facts mostly being people and incidents. Once we realize that we are, in truth, lords and masters, bestowers of value, shapers of the soft facts (there are no hard ones), then surely the art of life becomes something intensely creative. Morality becomes a real art instead of merely a question of principles. For a possibility opens. We can conquer life by bestowing what significance we choose upon the battle, down to its minutest detail. Every incident, situation, trouble, scare, difficulty, experience, hardship, is—what we make it. I knew a woman who could make the passing of the salt at table into a tragedy, and every error of every domestic servant into a quaking catastrophe. She made these things into tragedies. She could equally well have made them into comedies. Or better still have made them into nothings. We all exercise this power all our lives, this power of positively creating the facts, this power which Keyserling truly says is what Jesus meant by the Kingdom of Heaven within us.

It offers us a real philosophy of morality. It calls upon all our strength and courage and endurance and goodness, providing quite enough *battle* to satisfy any warrior. For, once we accept it as a method, once we dignify it with a name, the Philosophy of Significance, then we have material to work upon all our lives, we have a definite approach to each situation. We can take things well or we can take them badly, we can make mountains out of molehills or molehills out of mountains. The accident, the quarrel, the illness, the tiring effort, the sin, the disappointment, the failure, the impossible person, the insult, the delay, the crisis, are shaped and felt by us according to the significance we chose to bestow. "Is your present experience hard to bear?" wrote the inspired Edward Carpenter.[1] "Yet remember that never again perhaps in all your days will you have another chance of the same. Do not fly the lesson, but have a care that you master it while you have the opportunity." This is the creative crown that is placed upon Man's head. This is his nobility. Here lies his

[1]"Towards Democracy", (Allen & Unwin)

mastery. In this realm stretches the empire of his un-bloodied conquests. How high he can rise! With what radiance do the greatest of these achievements shine upon us and uplift our hearts! Rosa Luxemburg was cast into prison. But for that woman four walls did *not* a prison make. "This is my third Christmas in a cell" she wrote: "the sand crunches so hopelessly under the steps of the sentry that all the desolation and futility of existence rings from them in the damp, dark night. I lie there, quiet, alone, covered in the fourfold black cloth of darkness; weariness; bondage; winter; and at the same time my heart beats with an incomprehensible, unknown, inner joy, as if I were walking in radiant sunshine over a flowery meadow. And in the darkness I smile at life, as if somehow I knew the magic secret that all evil and sorrow lay defeated, changed into clear light and joy. And then I search myself for a reason for this joy, and find nothing, and am compelled to smile at myself again; I believe that the secret is nothing else but life itself; and the deep darkness of night is as beautiful and soft as velvet if only one sees it rightly. And in the crunching of the damp sand under the slow heavy steps of the sentry sings too a lovely little song of life if one only knew how to hear it rightly."[1] Thus do they live, thus do they write in whom the inexhaustible fountain of inward happiness rises from their kingdom of heaven!

Before leaving this power of significance, I would wish to safeguard myself against the sophist and the

[1] "Letters" in *Adelphi*.

extremist. The sophist will say that this is a skilful way of not facing facts. And a clever debater could certainly make it appear so. An able dialectician can do anything when the matter is subtle and the core is deeply buried. Think how easy it would be to wriggle away from one of the best exhortations ever made. "There are two ways of ridding ourselves of a thing which burdens us," said Huysmans, "casting it away or letting it fall. To cast away requires an effort of which we may not be capable. To let fall imposes no labour, is simpler, without peril, in reach of all. To cast away, again, implies a certain interest, a certain animation, even a certain fear; to let fall is absolute indifference, absolute contempt; believe me, use this method and Satan will flee." The sophist might persuade the inexperienced person that this is equivalent to turning our backs upon an unpleasant fact. For it is more or less equivalent to that. But there is a positive and negative way of doing everything. And no one can fail to see that there is a difference between turning our backs away from a fact pretending that it does not exist, and turning our backs while deliberately bestowing an insignificant value upon it. There is a difference between running away from the fact of sex and bestowing upon it little value if necessary or divine value when possible.

The extremist will object that this philosophy of living cannot always succeed—and he is only interested in the extreme cases. There are many poverty stricken people who could not possibly carry it out, there are marriages in which the incompatibility of the partners makes it impossible. And that is perfectly true. But because a certain method does not work in extreme cases, it is not therefore useless. The extreme case should be ruled out of all discussions.

XIII

I DO not possess sufficient psychological knowledge to say how far the approach to reality, as here indicated, could or should be part of our early education. The needs of the mind are so many and so complicated, its unfolding is so mysterious, that I, for one, could feel little confidence in advocating any measures for the teaching of adolescents. Possibly schoolmastering belongs to the list of insoluble problems. It is easy to say that it is an art, and that perpetual improvization practised by the artist-schoolmaster will provide each boy with what he needs at the moment. But how many such artists can we expect to find, knowing their scarcity in any profession? However, luckily most of us can say with Herman Melville: "I date my life from the age of twenty-five." He meant that he then woke up to the possibility of creative advance from experience-knowledge. We must learn to make that advance—or die. When we are younger than twenty-five we have experiences of ecstasy more frequently. That is the great reward of youth. One might almost say that youth is inspired and upheld by the sheer ecstasy of youth itself. That is why every young girl or man frequently feels that he can overcome the whole world and has no equal on the earth. That is why each writes poetry then, and why, to each, that poetry seems so very good. That is why, however terrible it may be to be young it does not matter, for we are inspired, not with wisdom but with life. That is why artists when they are young survive the disappointments and blows and disillusions of their campaign. That is why so many people think that nothing can make up for the loss of youth. Something does fade, some light does go out. There was a time when things seemed otherwise! we cry. "There was a time," said Wordsworth in his sad, tremendous way, "when meadow, grove, and stream, The earth, and every common sight, To me did seem Apparelled in celestial light." "There was a time," said Coleridge in the most mournful of all poems, "when, though my path was rough, This joy within me dallied with distress, And all misfortunes were but as the stuff Whence Fancy made me dreams of happiness." "There was a time," said Ruskin, "when I experienced a feeling of Sanctity in the whole of Nature from the slightest thing to the vastest. These feelings remained in their full intensity till I was eighteen or twenty, and then, as the reflective and practical power increased, and 'the cares of this world' gained on me, faded gradually away in the manner described by Wordsworth." It is frightfully real—the lament contained in the words of those great men. Each was an extreme example of a universal problem; each grew miserable as he grew older, Ruskin even crying out at the last—"no bird sings, or will sing for me for evermore!"

We all come to that river. How to cross it—and at the other side regain new life? All we want is to keep growing. That is our most intense desire: for if only we can keep growing then we can keep awake and alive and even happy perhaps. To keep growing—that seems to me the root of the matter. It is amazing how easy it is to die by mistake. It is so easy to let one's sense of beauty and wonder go rusty. I confess personally that I have often just not enjoyed lovely and wonderful sights around me because of financial worries.

Yet we have it in our power—provided our circumstances are not extreme—to keep awake and for ever enriching ourselves. This can be done by *allowing* our intuitional gleams full scope, by never failing to open ourselves to the influences of the universe, by yielding, by sitting still, by taking in, by accepting, by beholding this earth and beholding it well.

It is then that we find ourselves using the intellect with joy and creative advantage. It is then that all the activities of the mind fall into place: disputation through Logic, speculation through Philosophy, investigation through Science, and revelation through Art.[1] Thinking from a central experience ourselves we are in no danger of getting mixed up amongst those activities —rather it is our privilege to watch out that the exponents do not get thus muddled. We hold a key, we have received a clue; and only now therefore can we possibly appreciate the highest expressions of Art— which in one form or another symbolizes the deepest experience of the Divine. In a word, we will always be interested, we can never be bored. People sneer at reading. And sometimes it is a sound thing to sneer at.

[1] "Farewell to Argument," J. S. Collis (Cassell)

194

But if we can read with real understanding then it is as fine an activity as any other—and quite as creative. For those who know how to read—I say this deliberately knowing all there is to know concerning the dangers of reading, and having heard all there is to hear about "living" as opposed to "reading," and being sick to death with that conventional prating, and every day more and more sick to death with conventional high-brow remarks—for those who know how to read, for those who know how to keep watch over the unfolding of everlasting sorrow and everlasting joy, there is the reward of permanent growth and the peace of vision; for them there can be no winter of desolation nor any quenching of the flames from the fire of life.

XIV

IT is hard to see how England can survive as a country in which people can live without going mad, unless a new conception (however really old) of the Divine is embraced and a philosophy of living agreed upon. The saddest thing about England to-day is its lack of social life, of community. There used to be circles of community. The Machine like a shell has shattered circles both small and large. There is no circle at all—narrow or broad. Everyone can go anywhere and see everything. Everyone can communicate physically to an unheard of extent. But psychically there is less communication than in the whole of recorded time. Yet this is what we desire above *all*: friends, personal relationship, love. If we have these things we can almost dispense with the motor car. If we love our neighbour we can almost do without the radio. We burn for this. For this we labour and fight. We must have it! There must be a communion of souls —whether saints or sinners. There is joy in Germany to-day. There is joy in Russia. Not for all. But for many. For those who have now a communion of work, of purpose, of ideals, and therefore of fellowship and of hearts. No doubt this was brought to birth in the one case by the humiliation of a great people, in the other by overwhelming oppression. England is not in similar case. Must we pray for the whip of humiliation? Must we pray for a violent revolution? Both things would awaken England. Neither will come. But slow decay will come unless we have a revival of the religious spirit. A moral movement such as Buchmanism is so utterly, utterly lacking in spirituality and knowledge of the Divine, that when we place the wretched farce of its religious aspect (its moral aspect is excellent) beside any religious movement in the past, we get a truly terrible symbol of the emptiness and ignorance of this educated day! Yet such a movement proves again and again the need for communion. It is *the* need. There are only two ways of getting it: by upheaval or by religion. "I always believe in having Whist Drives," said a parson to me recently, "for it brings people together." That was the best he could think of. It did not occur to him that the introduction of religion into his parish would bring people together—the very word religion means a "binding." People join together with most advantage when they join together in their knowledge of God. My own way of stating that in this essay has been crude. But crude and earthly though my words have been I have gone no further than saying that God is love; I have done no more than affirm again that the feeling of new life and joy surging up within us when we receive intuitional gleams is itself salvation and liberation—that it is all we have of surety, and quite enough. Might we not join together on this central experience and see what we can build?

IV
EDUCATION
H. W. HECKSTALL-SMITH

Dedicated
to
J. J.

I

What Does It Mean?

BY Education I mean the process by which the young become fitted (or unfitted) for the time when they will be grown up, and will have to take their place as responsible members of the community.

All the higher animals educate their young by protecting them, and preparing them for the inevitable adventure of fending for themselves.

Though I start with this definition, I do not regard it, or any other definition, as final or complete. In some abstract subjects definition can properly be used as a signpost, but not as a boundary. Electrical resistance, and the knight's move in chess, can be exactly defined, but happiness and religion cannot. In Mathematics, which we invent for ourselves, we can define our terms exactly; but in the world we find waiting for us (and have to cope with somehow) definition can hardly be more than something to go on with, though we must attempt it to clarify our own thinking and make it intelligible to others. My definition of Education gives a starting-point, but not a limit.

One of the best schoolmasters I have ever known got mixed up with the problem of whether a little boy, playing football on a cold day, should wear a sweater or not.

In the backwash of this eddy he remarked bitterly to me: "I don't know whether I'm a nursemaid or what." As I didn't know either, I suggested that we two, and anyone else on the staff who wanted to join us, should try to find out.

A series of fortnightly discussions followed, in which we tried to discover what we were aiming at; and after about twelve hours' work, spread out into five sessions, we arrived at conclusions which still seem to me useful in clearing the ground. Here they are:—

The first aim of education is to protect the young from death or disaster due to elementary ignorance.

The second aim of education is to develop the latent or growing powers of the individual as an individual.

The third aim of education is to develop the latent or growing powers of the individual as a member of Society.

The first aim, protection, is obvious to anyone who has had a baby. A baby wants to pick up a red-hot coal or eat mud, and you can neither explain to him nor let him do it. If you were not there, or he could do what he liked, he would die; and that settles the question of complete freedom in education.

The second and third aims, development as an individual and as a social being, I can best explain by a fable:—

A baby once met a cat for the first time. The cat had a beautiful bushy tail which waved enchantingly within reach. The baby wanted to see if he could grasp this beautiful thing by reaching for it. He wanted to find out what it felt like to touch. He wanted to see what happened if he pulled it. With great joy he reached out, seized the tail, and gave a pull. The cat, in self-defence, at once turned and scratched the baby, and the baby cried, having had some education as a social being.

In grasping, touching and pulling the cat's tail the baby was getting on with his education as an individual by practising these things, and this part of his education gave him great pleasure. But the social part of his education gave him pain.

The three aims take turns in being the most important. Protection is the most important for the newborn child; self-development only begins about six weeks later when the child begins to take notice, and social development begins when he recognizes his father and mother as people outside himself.

As the child gets older the necessity for protection very slowly diminishes, while the importance of self-development very slowly increases, and becomes paramount during the nursery-school and infant-school periods.

A child takes the first big step in his social development when he makes contact with other children.

In the long approach to maturity the need for protection should gradually fade out, and the need for social development does in fact become paramount.

(Some people damage both themselves and others

throughout long lives through quite elementary ignorance. A young child may burn himself, or the household, through elementary ignorance about matches; and marriages can be ruined through elementary ignorance about sex or food.)

Self-development never fades out, but social development grows past it. To expect social development, specially in the sense of conscientious helpfulness, too early in a child's life, does a lot of harm. Young children can be helpful for fun, making a game of it, but must not be expected to be helpful as a matter of duty.

A successful education allows the emphasis to change from protection to self-development, and from self-development to social development, at the right speed.

Protection, self-development, and social development inspire deep instinctive needs at different times of life. The feeling of a need for protection is stronger in the infant, and in the pre-adolescent and the adolescent the needs for self-development and social development seem to alternate. They do not rule together, but they take turns at ruling. An adolescent throws himself with fierce energy now into woodwork, and now into being in the football team. If he has to do one when he wants the other, there is often an equally fierce resistence, and there is nearly always an equally fierce resistence against protection, which (he feels) should now be finished with. But during the whole period of education all three needs have to operate; and for this reason it cannot all be pleasant.

It is here that it seems to me the Free Schools may make a serious mistake. They assume that all will be well if children can always do what they want to do at the moment. In assuming this they assume that all the strife and difficulty of adolescence come from the outside, whereas really the strife is within and inevitable.

The heat in the eternal discussion, as to whether children should be forced to do things or allowed to do what they like, is largely a rage round a false problem or a misunderstanding. A famous Don at Oxford once said: "It doesn't matter what a boy is taught so long as he doesn't like it"; and many progressive schools now say: "It doesn't matter what a boy learns so long as he likes it."

The conscientious conservative and the conscientious progressive are both wrong, as usual; and as usual each has a considerable lump of right on his side.

If a subject or an activity at a school is disliked, it may mean that it is being done badly by the authorities, or it may not.

On the whole, I think that self-development gives the adolescent the keenest pleasure for the longest time; and self-developing activities which are disliked should be strongly suspected of being wrong in the sense of being either badly arranged or useless for the particular child who dislikes them.

Learning to do mathematics or carpentry, to sail a small boat, to play games like tennis or fives or chess, to play the piano, develop you as an individual if you like them. If you dislike them, either they are badly taught or else you personally are unsuited for them. One should not be satisfied with a state of affairs in which you go on doing them and disliking them.

Social activities, though they are best for you if you enjoy them, may still be good for you if you dislike them. And you may rightly have to put up with protection at times, however much you hate it.

If you take the general view of education as the development of the individual and social powers, plus such protection as is needed, you will agree that any attempt to graft on qualities or powers from outside is bound to fail, and may very well cause trouble and waste by preventing the development of what is really there.

Any attempt to produce a particular type is therefore wrong, because it denies the life from within.

The duty of educators is to provide the opportunities and the environment which make growth possible.

II

The World We Live In

HUMAN beings are still in a primitive and ill-adjusted state. Their brains, and their technical powers over the external world, have run rapidly ahead of their emotional lives, their religion and their understanding of themselves.

We need not be unduly depressed by this, if we realize our extreme youth as a species, and the very small part of our time as a species during which we have been in any sense civilized. Probably we have gone too fast for the last five thousand years and got out of gear.

I remember calculating that if the history of the earth, since it came off the sun, were written in the twenty-five volumes of the *Encyclopædia Britannica* with the time equally spaced throughout the history, one letter would represent about ten years. One word would stand for the life of a man.

Each of the twenty-five volumes has more than 1,000 pages of 144 lines in double column.

On this scale, the last six volumes would give the history since the earliest easily traceable geological strata, the Cambrian, were laid down. We know that life began earlier than this, but we do not know how much earlier. The Trilobites, whose fossils appear in the Cambrian, were very complex forms of life, and therefore the history of life itself must be much longer than this. One thousand million years—twelve volumes —is a recent estimate.

The last four lines of the last column of the last page of the last volume would give us our history since rather before the birth of Christ. The last twenty lines would give us the history of what might reasonably be called Civilization (as far as we know).

The first man-like creatures would probably appear in the history not earlier that twenty pages from the end of the last volume. It is no wonder that we are in a mess (or, if you prefer it, that we have not got anything like straight yet).

This mess has long been recognized. The Psalmist says: "Lo, I was born in sin, and in sin hath my mother conceived me," but "Lo, I was born in a muddle, and in a muddle hath my mother conceived me," seems to me nearer the truth.

The Church's doctrine of Original Sin may be understood in various ways. It may be simply the expression of a feeling of disgust and shame about sex. "Better not to marry, but better to marry than burn," as St. Paul said, giving himself away generously though unintentionally.

It may be the idea that everyone has a strong twist in the direction of evil, which must be whipped out of him in childhood. "Be pure in heart, boys, or I'll flog you till you are," as the famous Dr. Keate is reputed to have said at Eton.

Both these ideas have been unqualified disasters for humanity. At every turn we met their results in our educational system to-day, still producing horrors.

Though these interpretations are nightmare errors, it is not for nothing that the Church holds the doctrine of original sin.

For some reason that we do not yet understand, people left to themselves do tend to go wrong. "Video meliora proboque, deteriora sequor."

They go wrong both as groups and as individuals. Animals in general do not. A normal lion is a "good" lion, but for humans there appears to be no norm. For lions the problem of evolution has been comparatively simple, but humans, attempting a much more difficult job, have got into a mess. The brilliant fable of the Garden of Eden accounts for this by the definite intervention of an external agency; but this does not seem to me a satisfactory solution. I am not concerned (nor am I able) to tackle this central problem of humanity here; I am only concerned to point out the danger of deterioration as a fact.

The proof that humanity does go wrong is that it has. It is not enough to point out that now children are corrupted by their elders, who in turn were corrupted by their elders, and so back to antiquity. The advance of our technical powers without a corresponding advance of spiritual powers is not enough to account for our troubles, for they existed before the big technical advances.

There seems to be a sort of innate incompetence which we must cope with if we are not to perish. Possibly, instead of saying there is something wrong, we should say there is something missing; some extremely important factors we have almost entirely neglected.

I can suggest briefly what these factors are. One is the powerful group of primitive instincts which really control many of our activities. Some psychologists are now finding out about them, and we shall not be able to cope with them or use them to help us until not a few but many of us understand them. There is now being run a race between psychology and ignorance, with the survival of humanity as the prize.

The other is what Quakers call the Inner Light. It has been known throughout human history, and given many names. The first of these factors may be either an ally or a destructive enemy, according to whether it is understood or denied. The second is an ally ignored, a power not used.

The view that humanity does somehow tend to go wrong does not oppose the idea underlying Homer Lane's successful method of treatment of delinquent children at the "Little Commonwealth"; the idea that evil comes from impulses capable of good use, but somehow misdirected. The method (which is also that of the child guidance clinics) is only useful if it is applied not coldly and impersonally but with a fundamental personal sympathy. The method of Jesus with the young man who had great riches is an example of it.

Many churchmen do now take a modified view of original sin. I feel sure they are leaving the original doctrine of the Church, and are taking a path along which they are forced by the pressure of facts.

Whatever the causes, the world of humanity is in a bad mess, and we and our children have to live in it, and if possible clear it up as we go.

Let us consider the nature of this mess, for it is relevant to the problem of what is to be done about education.

Mankind practically throughout the world is riddled with physical disease. Most of it is directly traceable to stupidity and wrong living. Even the splendid savage is largely an illusion. Though there are healthy savage races among those who have not made contact with civilized food and amusements, many savages are physically worse off than the rickety children in a Manchester slum.

Any traveller in England can see that most English people have unhealthy postures and unhealthy complexions, suffer from constipation and other functional diseases, particularly the diseases due to wrong food and shortage of air and exercise. Most English people have been allowed to grow up into what have been well called "physical illiterates," and many might have been called psychological cripples also.

Many of the child-guidance clinics have had to close their waiting-lists, though they well know that most adolescent delinquencies, such as stealing and sexual vagaries, can generally be cured by sympathetic and experienced treatment. The numbers that need treatment are so great that the clinics can only touch the fringe of the problem.

The Harley Street psychologists only keep their practices in bounds by charging enormous fees: thus rightly ensuring their livelihood while they give as much time as they can afford to the clinics.

The advertisements in the newspapers show how fear-ridden we are. Advertisements must pay. What they appeal to is real: fear of constipation, fear of growing old, fear of being ugly, fear of B.O., fear of all the things in the long lists at the bottom of those advertisements headed "Inferiority Complex."

I am not, of course, saying that fear is in itself bad. Without fear of real dangers we should perish. But many advertisements profit by widespread pathological fears, and are a proof of the enormous scale on which such fears exists.

Few English people in their short and inadequate holidays pursue living active pleasures. Most want something passive, when they have only to sit still and watch.

I have read that in mediaeval Europe, when much of the food was bad and monotonous, the spice trade boomed because spice enabled people to tolerate what would have been intolerable without it.

Many of us are worse off now, for we want spice with our whole lives.

I do not want to do more than suggest that there is a good deal wrong with the world. That this should be true is not a reason for despair. But we must allow for what is true. The major evils of war, danger of war, slums, unemployment causing despair and destitution, conditions as they now are in many industries, are both outward and visible signs of profound sickness of the spirit, and the breeding-ground of more and worse sickness.

It seems, therefore, that other tasks, not proper to it, are thrust upon education: the task of making it somehow possible for children to grow to maturity in a world of spiritual cripples, and yet remain healthy; and the task of making them able to help to cure the world of its spiritual and material diseases.

Let us consider what actually happens now about education. Think of yourself as wondering what to do about the education of a healthy, happy child now one year old.

Up to nursery school age the problem is a personal one. From nursery school age to seven the problem is to find a nursery school at all. After seven there is a choice of evils. Every kind of school has got something horribly wrong with it which knocks it out of the list of possibles for me. I feel as if I knew I had to live in one of a number of towns, and then found that the people in the first town were specially liable to typhus, those in the second to phthisis, in the third to cancer, and so on through the entire list, with the strong probability of a fatal disease in every town, special to that town.

The towns represent to me not the individual schools, but the kinds of schools. All kinds have something right about them, but to me it seems that each kind has something appallingly, and perhaps fatally, wrong. In part V. I return to this aspect.

III

Young Children

IF you want to grow up healthy, you should be born of healthy stock. Your parents should be healthy and sensible, and should love each other. I know this implies that they also should have been well-born and have grown up well; but I have to consider the best we can do with things as they are. Healthy stock is difficult to define; and it is wrong to be hopeless about children of unhealthy or unloving parents, or about children brought up in apparently hopeless surroundings.

The children may overcome these difficulties, but it is unusual for them to do so; and the statement at the beginning of this section is in general true.

Nursery schools do not begin to affect a child less than two years old. Yet the most important part of a child's education, the part with the most effect on the future, is the part when child and mother should not be separated. It is the nine months from conception to birth, and the two years after birth.

During the whole of this time the mother should be happy, healthy, and as far as possible free from anxiety if the child is to have a fair chance. She must live a regular, but not exciting life, among friendly people. A mother living the wrong kind of life during these three years is as dangerous to the community as a motorist driving recklessly through a town.

We can, and should, leave to the individual complete freedom in things that mainly concern the individual, but in things which vitally concern others who cannot help themselves, and where there is a general agreement about the right course to pursue, we cannot leave the matter to the individual conscience, or the control of economic forces, without disaster. We now do so, with the results that may be expected.

There is practically complete agreement about the sort of life the expectant mother should lead. All doctors, maternity nurses, and successful parents say much the same things. But these things are only done in the small minority of cases.

The agreement is not so complete about the life of mother and child during the child's first two years. But the differences are not so serious as for later ages. If a young mother consulted two doctors, chosen at random, independently, they would probably advise régimes with important differences, but either régime would probably give her child a much better chance than most children have now.

You may think I am dealing with health instead of education. If you do, consider again the definition that education is the process of fitting the young for adult responsibility. From this definition it follows that the most important part of education is the period from conception to when the child is about two years old. On this period, most of all, depends whether the child is ever fit for adult responsibility at all.

During this period the mother must be, as I have said, happy, healthy, clear of overpowering anxieties, and living in a friendly atmosphere.

If it is physically possible, the child must be breast-fed for the first nine months.

The mother must eat enough of the right sort of food, but not too much. (I should like to explain about the right food now, but if I began I should go on too long, and repeating what is easy to discover although it is generally ignored. Anyone who really wants to find out about food can now do it easily. People who do not find out have probably become, without knowing it, too dispirited to want to live.) She must not be too mathematical about it, but must eat what she likes, and have plenty of variety. Plenty of variety is possible even if one is careful to exclude the wrong things and include the right ones.

She must have fresh air and exercise every day and she must have leisure to do things she enjoys for fun.

An expert maternity nurse must be available for a short time before birth and some weeks after it. If the child is born in a hospital, the living conditions for the nursing staff in the hospital must be good, or the maternity nurse will probably be bad-tempered.

It may require a major revolution in the hospital system to make living conditions reasonable for the nursing staffs. It will probably mean an enormous increase in the pay of nurses, a large reduction of their working hours, longer holidays, with the dates fixed long enough in advance to allow the nurses to make arrangements, much better accommodation, and com-

217

plete freedom in free time. These reforms in turn will require the abolition of the voluntary system of raising money and the substitution of State support or maintenance by local authorities.

It may also mean the abolition of most of the big hospitals, which get mechanical like all big institutions, in favour of a large number of small hospitals, small enough for their whole medical, nursing and domestic staffs to know each other well, and, in good living and working conditions, to be on friendly terms with each other. There must be some big hospitals because many diseases need special and expensive equipment; but wherever possible hospitals should be small.

The physical and emotional state of the maternity nurse has an enormous effect on both mother and baby.

For the first two years of the child's life the mother must do the whole job, aided wherever possible by the father. The mother's circumstances must allow her to do this. Mothers only rarely now take full and proper charge of their children in the first two years of life. The poorer ones, specially in towns and in remote country districts, are prevented by their physical circumstances from having time, energy, space or material necessities for the job. Richer mothers, oppressed by social habits and engagements, leave their children in charge of nurses and so lay the foundations of psychological disaster. The best children now come from homes in which (the first necessity and, I suppose, a matter of luck) the mother and father love each other, and have enough money to have reasonable material surroundings, but not enough to pay a children's nurse. The next best come from poor but not hopelessly poor, homes in healthy surroundings, and the worst from those condemned by poverty and our industrial system to live in abominable physical conditions, and from the very rich who think they have little time to spare for their children.

Morning and afternoon sleep in the open air almost every day is most necessary from very soon after birth. The weather can be as cold and wet as it likes, but this does not matter so long as the rain or snow does not actually fall on the child. The air must get straight at the child from all sides, and he must not be in a deep pram, or, except for short emergencies, in a pram with the hood up.

When he is sleeping in the daytime he must be in the open air, away from people, and in silence. At night he must be in a different room from his parents, but within earshot, from at least nine months old, and preferably before.

Quite enough is known about children's food after weaning for the feeding to be done as it should be, by anyone who takes the trouble to find out about it.

Cow's milk is, in general, not safe at first, but many children's dried milks and special foods, unlike many of the patent foods for adults, are safe, and contain the right proteins and vitamins. The mineral salts can be got from fresh vegetables properly cooked (which means conservatively cooked).

But the patent foods are expensive, and the mashed vegetables take a lot of time and energy, and are rather expensive too. Both the time and the money necessary are out of reach of very many mothers now. Yet the children should have them.

In the second year of the child's life, when he can walk, he must have a clean, airy playroom to walk in, with a big enough variety of playthings in it to allow him to get on with his self-education. He must have a watchful and sensible adult handy, but must be protected from the wrong sort of adult.

Adults who are quite tolerable to (and indeed must be tolerated by) the parents, may be most dangerous to the young child. Anyone who is assertive, domineering, over-affectionate, anxious for affection, frigid, frightened of affection, or for any reason incapable of observant and sympathetic negligence, must be kept away from all young children, as if these complaints were infectious (or perhaps it is better to say because they are infectious).

Children cannot always be protected from unbalanced adults. There are so many about, especially among teachers and clergy, that it is most important that children should learn to mix with them and be strong enough to resist corruption.

But the strength to resist is not acquired by beginning very early. If you are convalescent after a serious strain and ardently wish to do a twenty-mile walk as soon as possible, you will do it quickest by being careful not to overtax your strength at the beginning. If you want to do your walk forty days from now it may be wrong to walk half a mile to-day, a mile to-morrow, a mile and a half the next day, and so on, for you may collapse before ever you reach the twenty-mile standard. It may be better not to walk more than a few yards for the first twenty days, and simply wait for strength.

In the same way children must be protected from dangers until they are strong enough to cope with them, and ill-adjusted adults are among their most serious dangers.

(I must make it clear that ill-adjusted adults are only necessarily a danger for very young children. At a later age some ill-adjusted adults are often most helpful to children strong enough to accept the good and avoid the bad in them. Nearly all of us look back on at least one teacher as having been a very special help in adolescence; and these specially good ones are often maladjusted in a special way which may spoil their own lives but does not prevent them from being useful to others.)

An extremely important fact, particularly for the later development of the child's social attitude, is that the father must take his part in the early years. Not only must the mother breast-feed the baby for the first nine months, and do all the baby-work of feeding and washing herself, (not employing a nurse if it can possibly be avoided), but the father must do his share of bathing, feeding, nappy-changing, playing, and all the rest of it.

The baby must find it natural to have both father and mother handy, to talk to and show things to, from as early as he can remember, if he is to grow up capable of co-operating with others in general, and feeling comfortable with both men and women.

It is specially important that neither mother nor

father should side-step the dirty work. The socially distinguished mother, who likes to see her children only when nurse has done all the tough jobs and the children are clean and presentable, is a public danger.

Many fathers have jobs which leave them neither time nor energy to help with the children.

If we don't want to go on having a C3 nation, such jobs must go.

When the Government wants to recruit for the Army it discovers (apparently with a shock of horror) that a very large proportion of possible recruits are physically a very poor lot. It then attempts to raise the standard suddenly by a combination of physical training in schools and moral exhortation. Both have come too late.

A good education must then be founded on the following things:

(*a*) Good health and heredity in the parents.

(*b*) Affection between the parents.

(*c*) The right sort of life for the mother, specially during the nine months before birth and the nine months after it.

(*d*) Breast-feeding for the first nine months.

(*e*) Mother, rather than nurse, doing the whole job personally for the young child.

(*f*) Father doing his share of this work.

(*g*) Fresh air, rest, the right sort of food, the right sort of playroom, and protection from the wrong sort of adult for the child.

There is nothing remarkable in all this. Sensible parents see that their children have it unless poverty handicaps them. But it is necessary that the State should really do its best to see that all children have it, for the lack of it causes damage that can never be repaired, though it can be alleviated, by later education.

It is the Government's most important job to see that all children get a satisfactory start. It is a matter that can no more be left to the private conscience than can the driving of cars or the selling of milk. The State cannot allow dangerous driving or the selling of tuberculous milk. Still less can it afford to allow children to be given the wrong sort of start, when there is general agreement about the nature of the right sort.

I have pointed out that the necessary right conditions for mother and children from the moment of conception till the child is two years old require a complete reform of the working conditions in Hospitals. Clearly other reforms are needed just as much, particularly in slum-clearance.

In January 1936, at a fire in an industrial area, a mother and eight children were burnt to death. All, with the father, were sleeping in two rooms. The father, mother and five younger children were sleeping in one room, and the three older children in one bed in the other room. There is nothing unusual in these conditions. But we realize them more clearly when they are the cause of a frightful tragedy.

Less dramatically, they are the continual cause of an unending series of tragedies no less frightful.

Linked with the slum-problem is the problem of malnutrition the extent of which is at last being realized; but it is still important to emphasize the wrongness of two commonly held views.

First, it has been supposed that to move people out of slums into good houses in good surroundings gets one a long way towards the solution of the problem of bad health in slums. This idea has been definitely disproved by the large-scale experiment in Stockton-on-Tees, an account of which is given in Chapter VII of "Poverty and the Public Health."[1] This book makes it quite clear that the part of the population who shifted to the new estate with good houses was definitely worse off in health than the part which stayed in the slums because (as it has been graphically put) "the extra rent came out of the children's bellies." Shortage of food through poverty is thus shown to be a worse danger than slums.

Secondly, it has been supposed that malnutrition is largely due not to food-shortage through poverty, but to ill-balanced diets, modern highly refined foods, and bad cooking. This is sometimes true. Rich people can suffer from malnutrition. But it is definitely wrong to suppose the main trouble is due to anything other than food-shortage through lack of money.

It is the definite opinion of Dr. M'Gonigle and Mr. Kirby, as the result of a most detailed investigation extended over many years, that the average housewife knows quite enough about food-values and cooking to get on pretty well so long as she can actually buy enough food.

(Scene, an industrial area in 1936: "No, we don't eat much on Thursdays.")

[1] G. C. M. M'Gonigle and J. Kirby, 1936.

Sir John Orr has estimated that 10,000,000 of the 45,000,000 population of Great Britain live at or below the threshold of adequate nutrition; and Dr. M'Gonigle claims quite definitely that this estimate is too low.

I strongly suspect that there is still lurking in the minds of a good many people the feeling that those who suffer severely from poverty have sinned and are getting the punishment they deserve. This seems to me first an error and secondly an evil point of view. Even if it were true and right it would not apply to children born helplessly into these conditions. "The sins of the fathers are visited on the children," is interesting solely as a statement of objective fact. It does not represent what it is sometimes taken as representing—a moral point of view. It has nothing whatever to do either with the religion of Christ or with any reputable ethical systems. No one can defend it as a motto for conduct.

Yet I think it is still active, with "eye for eye, tooth for tooth," and other similar Old Testament slogans, in the minds of many official Christians with a Bible-Christian background.

I suggest that if such conditions as these, and the conditions of working in the hospitals, and the other innumerable indirect causes of waste of lives of infants, either by causing death or by producing physical or psychological cripples, were recognized during a war as a danger to the nation, they could be quickly changed; no less quickly than factories making other things were changed to munition factories in the Great War.

The first charge of all on the Government is to see by all the means in its power that all mothers and children are in what are known to be the right physical conditions from the moment of conception till the child is two years old; and anything whatever which gets in the way must be dealt with as a national danger.

The problem looks insoluble with the slums and industrial conditions as they are now; but it is not more difficult as a piece of social engineering than it was to produce and maintain a well-armed, well-trained, well-fed army of two million men on foreign soil.

That was done when we were convinced that the nation could not survive unless it was done. This can be done when we realize that the nation must remain in a C3 category until it is done.

The difficulty of tackling this major problem is of two distinct sorts.

First, there is the mechanical difficulty. This, though severe enough, is no more severe than was the military problem in War-time.

Second, there is the difficulty of intention. This is that people who are well off, and *a fortiori* those in authority, do not really feel it is important enough. There was something dramatically attractive in the raising and equipping of our gigantic Army in War-time; and, still more important, there was personal glory for its leaders. This business of seeing that young children have a fair chance in life is not dramatic; it can lead to no honoured place in a victory procession.

Education depends most of all on the pre-natal life of the mother and on the very early years of the child. At present, the chance of a good education is often gone for ever, long before the child goes to school.

This problem is not being solved because there is not at present enough really serious intention to solve it in the hearts of those in authority.

It is interesting to note the rise of general prosperity which immediately followed the rearmament in 1936. It suggests that if the Government had been willing earlier to finance public work in slum clearance, road-building, school-building, and other things that affect general health, this improvement might have come earlier. The Government can see national strength in terms of mechanical arms, but not in terms of healthy children.

IV

The Disagreement of Experts

WHERE experts agree, one can generally accept their views with confidence; where they disagree one must accept all views with caution, and do one's best to form an unprejudiced opinion.

Where experts disagree in Science, they are usually in friendly touch with each other; but in Education one of the great difficulties is that disagreeing experts lose touch with each other, and in general make little attempt at unprejudiced thinking.

I have not room to deal with more than one major example of disagreement and loss of touch among educational experts; but I will take one thing to show the importance of the general problem. If you compare the general attitude of educational theorists, for example, on such a fundamental matter as discipline (with which is bound up the whole problem of personal relationships) with that practised in most schools, particularly secondary schools, and preached by the Headmasters' Association and Headmasters' Conference, you can see that the difference is so great that each side regards the other as being so far wrong in the matter as to be not worth meeting in discussion.

It is sad that the theorists and the practitioners should part company completely, for neither side is the least likely to be completely right or completely wrong. Let me take one specific case. The Educational theorists, backed by most of the training colleges, and practically all the psychologists, probation officers and those practised in dealing with delinquent children, disapprove of corporal punishment. The Headmasters, with very few exceptions, approve it, backed by the tradition and experience of the public schools and the secondary schools. The pity is that the parties to the dispute do not try to convince one another. As things are going now, the Training Colleges will win in the end, for they will continue to turn out their students with their own ideas (on the whole), whereas the Headmasters will retire or die. But this will not affect the Public Schools for a long time, for they do not draw much on the Training Colleges, and they make no touch at all with the parts of the Universities that deal with the theory of Education. Secondary School Headmasters who are appointed direct from Public Schools will also be unaffected. But many of these are rebels who want a fresh start and are therefore in touch with the theorists.

I suspect all the arguments commonly used for and against corporal punishment. I need not repeat them, for they are well known; and most of them by now are alarm clocks at whose sound passion and prejudice awake and dash into the discussion. The reasons commonly given for it are true but unimportant—afterthoughts and rationalizations, not causes. **The** reasons commonly given against it are largely ideal, and tend to ignore experience.

I have known corporal punishment condemned on the grounds that (*a*) it means rule by fear and (*b*) it inhibited the spirit of adventure. Both these contentions seem to me untrue. I have known it defended by a headmaster in reply on the ground that boys are primitive and understand this sort of thing. This seems to me true; but it would have been truer if he had added that masters are equally primitive, for civilized man is largely controlled unconsciously by the fears and superstitions and desires that control primitives consciously. There seems to be ample anthropological evidence for this.

Both these views ignored the effect on the person who gives it. This is extremely important, specially if the person is an adolescent or an adult of arrested emotional development.

I think I can see some of the reasons that make corporal punishment work well in a way.

1. It is very commonly regarded as a test of manhood. A boy who takes a caning without flinching is regarded by himself and the others as having come through a test.

2. Most people, whether from their upbringing or for other reasons, have a deep sense of guilt, which is extremely painful, but can be assuaged by punishment. These are the people who "ask for it" and go on behaving badly (almost without meaning to) till they get it. Then, for the time being, they are happy. Adults do this as much as children, but they don't usually manage

to get caned. A caning is just the sort of dramatic punishment which comforts someone with a feeling of guilt.

But the trouble is that it saves the guilty person from
making the effort to get really all right. It makes the
sense of guilt tolerable.

3. The feeling of suffering with others—specially
suffering something dramatic—is a very strong tie, and
boys like being fond of one another. Dramatic punishments make strong friendships.

4. Humanity wants scapegoats. Every criminal who
is punished makes the respectable people feel even more
respectable. The boys who don't get caned at school
(now the majority instead of the minority) are just as
proud of not getting caned (though in quite a different
way) as the others are of taking a caning without
flinching.

5. Schoolmasters are often extremely conscientious.
They like to comfort themselves by feeling they have
done their best, and they wish to point to some definite action they have taken to deal with any particular
problem.

There is usually neither time nor knowledge enough
for a master to solve school problems. He does not
understand the underlying causes and has not time to
deal with them. If he can say "I have now punished the
boys concerned, and the matter is settled" he satisfies
(with ordinary luck) (a) his conscience, (b) parents and
governors and other members of the staff, (c) the boys
concerned and others. He avoids the horribly painful
feeling of being inadequate, and can retain his peace
of mind.

.If the trouble recurs, he can do the same again. If it does not recur, he can regard the cure as the result of his action (though in fact either the recurrence or non-recurrence may be due to quite other factors).

The main thing is that the master may be happier in his work and better able to avoid strain.

6. A very powerful group of primitive instincts in man can find expression through corporal punishment. A man who does not understand these instincts may get into a complicated emotional state and become an extremely inconvenient member of society is he has no outlet whatever.

The instincts are of two kinds. One is of a kind which can be satisfied by happy marriage, and the other I take to be some sort of primitive survival, which we can only control if we realize its existence.

The main point is that a schoolmaster who does not know much about himself and is not happily married, but has a very high moral sense and a strong sense of duty (a not uncommon type, specially in public Schools) may actually be more friendly, more reasonable, easier to live with, and better at his job if he can so arrange matters that he can inflict corporal punishment and at the same time satisfy his moral sense and his sense of duty.

A school containing many masters of this type may thus be a better school in many ways with corporal punishment than it would be with these same masters but without corporal punishment.

The disadvantage of this sort of harmony, however, is that it is obtained at a price.

The schoolmaster whose internal strains are relieved by corporal punishment may find the adjustments necessary for a happy marriage so difficult that he cannot make them, and he loses the chance of having the good general effect that a happily married person unquestionably has on the community. He will have compensated so efficiently that he no longer wants the real thing.

7. A Headmaster, like many other people in positions of conspicuous authority, has often got there as the result of very strenuous efforts. He does not get pushed into the position for his competence, like the civil servant or railway official. He must apply for the job, and apply very strenuously.

Now people who apply for a job very strenuously may do so to satisfy some compelling inner need. An inner need for a position of conspicuous authority is really a need for reassurance against a feeling of inadequacy. The origin of this feeling need not concern us here. Possibly it appears in an adult man because his mother did not love him enough when he was a baby.

The point here is that the position of the Headmaster judicially inflicting punishment with a cane is just the sort of position to comfort a person with an inner feeling of inadequacy. He is being just. He can be kind if he wants to, but from a considerable altitude. The other party to the transaction is in a position of absolute submission before him.

He is Jove wielding the thunderbolt, with the additional satisfaction of doing it "justly" and "mercifully."

If he does not now say: "This hurts me more than it does you," he can really and honestly think it. He can combine in himself the godlike attributes of terror, justice and mercy.

Now a feeling of inadequacy inexorably demands comfort. Without comfort its victim may become intolerable to live with. Given comfort, he may become quite a useful member of society.

In this way the power to inflict corporal punishment does quite considerably improve many existing Headmasters. It pours oil into the wounds of their emotions, and makes them much pleasanter and more useful members of society than they would be without it.

It is quite wrong to suppose that using the cane is ruling by fear. The good boys (fortunately) are not good through fear of being caned if they are bad, but for quite other reasons.

I have experienced schools that use corporal punishment and schools that do not. My very strong impression as a result of experience is that corporal punishment absolutely fails at what it claims to do, which is to maintain good discipline in the sense of obedience to rules; but that, in the existing stage of human development, it may have quite accidental but considerable good effects. But I think these good effects are of the kind that produce apparent good results on the spot, but may in the long run do harm.

Possibly the training-college authorities can avoid the difficulty of dealing with the real world as it is now, and the Headmasters are so rushed by the continual pressure of events that they first cannot, and as they get older, dare not launch out into the danger of any thinking that might alter their habits.

I should make clear here that it is my impression that Headmasters who are so rushed that they have no time to think are really afraid of thinking, and allow themselves unconsciously to get rushed in order to avoid the pain and inconvenience that would certainly follow any attempt to think.

The practitioner is more apt to look wrong than the theorist, but he is forced to be closer to humanity, and while doing things in themselves undesirable, may be in himself less wrong.

I am inclined to think that if there is direct damage done by corporal punishment it is almost entirely done to the character of the executioner, whether school-master, schoolmistress, or (in the Public Schools) prefect. Only very few people are so well adjusted in their emotional lives that they could give corporal punishment without suffering psychological damage. The harm done to the boys who are punished is, I think, mostly secondhand, in that they have to associate with adults who are worse corrupted than they need have been. (Nervous boys are harmed directly, of course. But most schoolmasters and some prefects are now sensible enough to avoid caning nervous boys.)

Boys are apt to get deeply interested in the subject, and spend a great deal of time for years talking and thinking about it, and so diverting energy into unprofitable channels. In a school where corporal punishment has been long established, the emotions about it on the staff, though deep-seated and intense, may be dormant. If a disapproving new Headmaster abolishes it forthwith, the deep-seated and intense emotions on the staff may find other and more dangerous channels which may wreck the school. The Headmaster, if he wants to do the best for the boys, may have to wait till the incurable members of the staff are retired or dead, and try to avoid engaging new incurables.

But I must not go on about this matter, though it is very important. What I want to emphasize is that most of the theorists and most of the practitioners disagree flatly and are making no attempt to come to terms; that this is a pity, for it is most improbable that either view as now stated is completely right; that the factors which really operate are very probably being ignored by both parties (who content themselves by hurling verbal bombs like "sadist" and "sentimentalist" at each other at long range); and that the futile state of things is typical of the many places where experts differ over education, in that they do not differ and discuss like scientists, but differ and refuse to discuss like angry children. (The practitioners are, on the whole, angrier children than the theorists, perhaps because they suffer worse when they go wrong.)

The absence of touch between theorist and practitioner in Education covers the whole field. With it goes an almost complete absence, particularly in Headmasters, of the power of making objective judgments. When they descend into the arena of discussion, it is from Mount Sinai with infallible commandments.

I suppose the outstanding central difficulty about

Education is that we really know nothing reliable about it. Almost everything we do and assert about it rests on the prejudices and personal emotions of educators. There is no objective test, as there is in science. Let me give an extract from a history-book of the future.

"In the sixteenth century A.D. science began, with the exact experiments of Galileo, and his deductions from them. Before then all that passed for science was false, since it depended on what individuals wanted to be true, and not on any care for truth itself. It is strange that in the next thousand years there was no corresponding development in Education, incomparably more important. The pursuit of truth as such had given to humanity such power through science that they all but destroyed themselves through its irresponsible use, before, nearly a thousand years after Galileo, education as we now understand it began. Until then practically all the vast educational machines followed methods that we now know to be useless and dangerous. Here and there, by accident or good luck, were sporadic and short-lived outbreaks of true education."

V

WHAT SCHOOL WILL YOU CHOOSE?

IN this part of my Essay I imagine myself choosing an actual school for a child, and considering the high lights, good and bad, of the various types of school.

In my experience, parents who bother much about the choice of a school do this. They look for an outstanding advantage or a fatal disadvantage.

I shall therefore consider the outstanding types of English school in turn.

1. *Nursery Schools*

The nursery schools are good. You have only to look in at one to see this. Their great fault is that there are far too few of them. There should be several hundred times as many as there are. Every child who is not one of a large family, or of a small community living in the country, should spend his days at one. These schools have the great advantage of not having inherited the vile traditions of large classes and payment by results.

Small children are also such a nuisance to those who don't like them that they get teachers who do like them. (Of course teachers who only like small children are pathological cases, and are dangerous). Nursery

238

Schools are good partly because the nature of small children tends to make the teachers who take charge of them friendly and sensible.

2. *Kindergartens and Infants' Departments of Elementary Schools*

These, again, are pretty good on the whole. The old and wicked Victorian methods with young children have more or less gone, knocked out by Froebel, Montessori, and the psychologists. The worst difficulties (and they are pretty bad) are in the buildings and the staffing. Incredible as it may appear, classes of forty infants are still quite common. There is not much wrong in the spirit. In fact, where anything is being done about the education of children from two to seven, it is being done better than for earlier or later ages. I am talking about school education, not home education and saying it is good in nursery schools by comparison with education in schools for older children. It is not, of course, good compared with what it might be.

3. *The Junior Elementary Schools*

Here the horrors begin. I see two material horrors and one spiritual. First, there are large classes of forty, fifty, and even occasionally sixty. The Board of Education is still forced by economy to allow forty per classroom in Elementary Schools and thirty per classroom in Secondary Schools.

Every experienced teacher knows that such classes are too large for individual attention or general discussion. There is a best size for every class, but it varies with the subject. Except for a lecture-lesson, which should be a rare event, I think it is safe to say that no class should be bigger than twenty; and an average of fifteen would be quite good.

Unfortunately, buildings will continue to be built on the thirty-forty basis for a long time. Probably we shall have to wait till the birth-rate falls before classes are the right size. But let us do our best to see that as the numbers of children fall the numbers of classes and teachers do not fall with them. The schools now have about enough classrooms and teachers for half the present number of schoolchildren. Unless public opinion allows the Board of Education to change its policy, the numbers of classes and teachers will fall with the child-population, and the present ruinous state of things will be maintained.

Next, there are bad school premises. These were well described by Miss F. Hawtrey in January, 1936, in the words which follow:

Only too often the cloakrooms are dark and crowded; stuffy coats and caps hang close together; the basins are small and stained. There is no hot water; there are bits of yellow soap and one towel, not for the class of 50, but for the whole school of 200 or 300 children; the towel is changed once a week.

The playground itself is as hideous as a prison-yard. It is covered with asphalt, surrounded by walls with iron-barred gates into the street; there is a shelter with a slate roof and iron supports in one corner—not a blade of grass, not a tree, not a leaf.

The most precious thing for the child to-day is not bricks and mortar, but grass, trees, flowers, running water, birds, and animals. Children spend their early years in a mechanized world. The natural exclamation of a child nowadays on seeing a gull in flight is: "Look, Mummy! it flies like an aeroplane."

Many of the present conditions were those which would produce a slave mind. They might serve if they wished to produce a race of men and women who, in a mechanized world, would feed machines.

Everyone knows about these dangerous conditions, and the successive Ministers of Education are doing their best to correct them, or to assist the Local Authorities to do so. I suppose we can only push on as fast as possible. But let it really be as fast as possible, not as fast as is convenient and let the new buildings be really good.

The spiritual danger comes with the Special Place Examination. It is assumed that a small proportion of the children at Primary Schools can profit from secondary education. As secondary education is now organized, this seems quite reasonable.

Secondary education normally begins at the age of eleven. Children who can profit from it are reasonably expected to have reached a certain standard in (a) intelligence and (b) knowledge. The examination is carried out by methods which vary with the Local Authority concerned. But these methods agree in

trying to test both intelligence and knowledge. The
more special places a school captures in the yearly
Examination, the more credit goes to the school
and the teachers. Here is the danger: for it means
that in many schools the children are crammed, and
suffer the inevitable physical, mental and spiritual
degradation that must be the result of cramming. You
can often see it in their faces.

There are two other spiritual dangers in the Junior
Elementary Schools, but both are common to the whole
of English education. One is that too many of the
teachers have either lost their savour, or grown up
without any. There seem to be two wrong sorts of
teacher: the sort that lives for teaching and becomes a
vampire on the children, and the sort that took to
teaching as a third-best because of the pay, the pension,
and the holidays. The vampire type is to be found in
the better-off schools. You can't vamp a class of
forty.

The training Colleges are doing their level best about
the danger of the third-best, but it will not be cured till
England is no longer a C3 nation.

The other danger is a more subtle one. Of all the
people who work in this world, those who need most to
be normal in their affections are those who deal with
children. All teachers, male or female, should be
emotionally capable of marrying successfully. Marriage
is in itself no help for this. Many married people are
incapable of successful marriage, and many unmarried
ones are capable of it.

In general, there is a rule of celibacy for women

teachers, but none for men teachers; and where this rule operates many most valuable teachers are lost.

It would be a good thing if more women teachers were either young people looking forward to marriage or mothers who had married young, seen their children off into the world, and found themselves left full of energy and vitality before they were fifty. These, if they were friendly and happy, would be the best teachers of all.

4. *Senior Elementary Schools*

These differ from the junior schools in certain important particulars. They have completely escaped the examination danger, and lack the spiritual oppression of the Special Place Examination, except that many of the children must have failed in the Special Place Examination, and some may be suffering from that blow. But much of the best work is being done in these freer schools; and much more will be done when the Hadow reorganization scheme is complete, and the school-leaving age is raised to fifteen.

The troubles with size of classes, buildings, teachers in general, and celibate women teachers, remain; and, heaven knows, they are enough.

5 and 6. *Preparatory Schools and Public Schools*

Preparatory Schools take children between the ages of seven and thirteen or fourteen, and send them to the Public Schools. They charge fees, often very big ones, and are extremely efficient in doing what they set out to do.

Their classes are small, their buildings are good, their staffs are on the whole keen and well-paid. But spiritually they are disastrous. (Here I forget my vow to stick to criticisms about which there is general agreement.)

They are disastrous first because they know what they want and get it. They set out to produce in their pupils the "correct" attitude of mind and the "correct" behaviour. If we know what our children are going to be like, they will be no better than we are, and England cannot stand people like us much longer, for she is already near enough to the edge of destruction. To push a child into a mould, even into the best mould the teacher can imagine, is the worst crime possible for the teacher.

There are other dangers.

Children at Preparatory Schools have their time carefully organized to make sure that they do not get into mischief.

When later they are thrown on their own resources they are helpless. I have been able to see the danger of this very clearly, in a long experience of a Public School followed by some experience running a house with some boarders in a Secondary School.

In the free time at the Public School the younger boys mooned aimlessly about the corridors unless they were turned out of doors. If they were, they mooned aimlessly about the grounds. In the Secondary School the boarders in their free time—and there was a lot more of it—always all had a job on hand, and wanted hardly any apparatus. If they had no job on hand, they could

—and invariably did—invent an endless succession of excellent games, and play them heartily. They had been to village Elementary Schools, and had not lost their natural spirit.

The disastrous thing that the Preparatory Schools share with the Public Schools, and with all schools that require big fees, is the segregation of the moneyed class from everyone else. This is bad in two quite different ways.

First, it keeps the well-off children in a special and artificial world, from the safe refuge of which "those others" seem hardly real. The whole picture of life as they see it is a false one.

Second, it isolates the culture, understanding and sympathy which have a good chance to grow up naturally in a home with a background of reasonable freedom from economic anxiety.

Everyone should have this; and I suppose will have it when we have learnt as much about distribution as we know about production; but only a few have it now.

Children with this good background can have an enormous effect on those who have missed it, if they are really in touch for a long time. Occasional contacts (as in Public Schools Missions to Boys' Clubs in the slums) are not an effective substitute. How often do both the lucky ones, and the unlucky, mistake for inborn virtue what is only the result of better luck!

The present inbreeding is a tragic loss, both to the children without a leisured background and to those with it. If only the children in the well-off schools were now spread evenly throughout the schools of England, what gainers both the children and the schools would be!

As things are, the defeatists, the people who have seen through everything and despaired, the people who are tragically forced back on "Let us eat and drink, for to-morrow we die" are coming from the preparatory and Public Schools.

6 and 7. *Public Schools and Secondary Schools*

(I use the terms as commonly understood. Strictly Public Schools are Secondary.)

I, who have moved to a Secondary School after ten years as a master in a very good and much-beloved Public School, have seen the differences between them very clearly.

The love one can feel for a Public School, however angry it makes one and however wrong one may think it, is a tremendous thing. Anyone who leaves a Public School after serving a long time as a master suffers a wound which may never heal. Even some of the boys feel this after their four or five years; but for a master the depth of the feeling is profound. Do not therefore expect reason from Public School Masters. They may have love, and possessive love casteth out reason. Regard them with respectful affection, but do not hope to change them. They cannot betray their gods, even if these gods do evil.

The Public School was full of the most charming defeatists—the people Shaw presented in *Too True to be Good*, (a phrase I had often used to myself in the years before the play was written).

In the Secondary School there was an anxious

struggle for jobs, but no defeatism. There was an obvious lack of the background of leisured appreciation of the good. When I talk about "appreciation of the good" or "good things" I am trying to express the good sense of the word "culture" without bringing in its bad associations. I can find no satisfactory word to replace it. I mean the background of leisured appreciation of books, music, poetry, painting, architecture, plays, sensitive and intelligent talk, which are only possible to households with a good enough standard of living to allow the proportion of leisure that everyone ought to have. If only a dozen of the Public School defeatists had been in the Secondary School, they would never have become defeatists, and the Secondary School, already even more lovable than the Public School, would have become capable of understanding good things it has never had a chance to realize.

The Public Schools, like the Preparatory Schools, work to produce a type they know in advance. They do not try so hard, and fortunately they are less successful, but they do try, with fair success; and so their way is the way of death. They produce conformers or rebels, but not free spirits, for conformers and rebels are equally in chains.

Perfect Pater. Marvellous Mater. Knock the critic down who
    dares——
Very well, believe it, copy, till your hair is white as theirs.
Yours, you say, were parents to avoid, avoid them if you please.
Do the reverse on all occasions till you catch the same disease.[1]

[1]W. H. Auden. Poems. (Faber & Faber.)

I think I should point out that the disciplinary system in the Public Schools, though it has grown less rigid and less sure of itself, has not really changed. It is very different from the kind of system approved by the Training Colleges and the psychologists. There is no doubt that the methods of the psychologists work well with delinquent children brought before the law courts (when they are given a chance). They certainly work well with the problem cases which are brought to the child-guidance clinics. I am not saying that either way is right and the other wrong; only that the gap is immense. Practically nothing is being done to bridge it.

Public Schools do give a training in the experience and management of really intense emotions. All kinds of most violent passions are continually roused, and those that experience them have to come to terms with them somehow. The trouble is that these passions are mostly abnormal, and their only value is that they give practice in intense feelings. They give very little training for the problems of the world outside school.

Suppose you couldn't ride a horse, but had to get right across England on horseback. You might train on the Grand National course. You would learn about falls and fear and jumps and speed but not about route-finding or how to cope with long monotonous stretches, or the care of the horse and yourself. Your training would be better than nothing but not nearly so good as it ought to be, or as it easily might have been if you had used a little common sense.

The Public School trains for some of the jumps and difficulties (but not all), and ignores everything else.

The Secondary School trains for some of the ordinary things, but not the jumps.

The outstanding evil in Secondary Schools is the immense pressure of the School Certificate and of the necessity of getting a job early. They suffer hideously from cramming, which the Public Schools, with their greater economic freedom, can avoid. That is partly why the Secondary School boys so often capture brilliant entrance scholarships at Oxford and Cambridge, crack up during their University career, and finish with poor degrees.

I think there are two other reasons for these breakdowns. One is the after-effects of partial malnutrition due to poverty in childhood, and the other the awful pressure of economic necessity. Those who must get a job or suffer severe poverty do not do themselves justice in a crucial test. The blow of failure, for a boy with a home which can support him in case of need, is to his pride. This is severe, but not so severe as unemployment and poverty.

Quite an important difference in the prospects of the Public School boy and the Secondary School boy comes from the fact that Public School men do occupy a great many of the key positions, and tend to confine jobs in their gift to Public School boys. Sometimes, but less often, the Secondary School boy is preferred as such for the same sort of reason. When either of these things happens it is a very regrettable result of the extremely clear-cut line of division between two groups of schools which are really in a sense doing the same job.

Secondary School discipline is, on the whole, like

Public School discipline, except that the seniors are bound to have much less power and responsibility. This is inevitable for two reasons: school time is shorter, and does not include the night and the week-end; and the proportion of eighteen-year-olds is very much smaller because so many must rush off for jobs when they are sixteen.

Nevertheless, the Secondary Schools stand with the Public Schools in their view of discipline.

Both pupils and staff in Secondary Schools suffer terribly (though they seldom know it) from the lack of a leisured background of appreciation of the good. This is a terrible loss, and nothing can replace it. It is extremely doubtful if the School Certificate, which is always driving them on to learn more and more things, is forcing upon them anything like the right choice. There is a large and growing body of opinion that the inevitable curriculum is pretty seriously wrong. It certainly tends to produce a thoroughly scrappy knowledge of a lot of things, without making the candidate reasonably safe in elementary English and arithmetic.

The Public Schools used once to teach two subjects thoroughly. One was Latin, and the other Greek or Mathematics. For all else they trusted in God.

This scheme, though open to fairly obvious objections, did at least leave its victim fairly clear about the difference between knowing a thing and not knowing it. If, later in life, he chose to learn something else (some sort of science, for example) he had a standard of sound learning.

If you take eight subjects in the School Certificate, and get three fails, three passes, and two credits (and a School Certificate), what sort of standard of learning are you likely to have? And what about the teacher who has rushed you through?

Secondary School children do not get a fair chance in the matter of health. Far too many of them arrive at the school with physical defects which are very difficult (and sometimes impossible) to rectify.

Physically they are not usually so bad as their parents, but to say this is not to praise them.

They have more physical defects than children at Preparatory Schools, because their food, living conditions, and chances of getting air and exercise have been worse; but they have fewer psychological defects because their parents are much less often divorced, separated, or at loggerheads, and probably had much more direct touch with them (through not being able to afford a nurse) in early childhood.

Both the Secondary Schools and the Public Schools are on the whole bad at physical education. With the establishment of Carnegie College, Leeds, they ought to begin to improve. Where there is any physical education at all, it is less amateurish in the Secondary Schools than in the Public Schools. But in one thing the Secondary Schools are far behind the Public Schools. They get much less fresh air and exercise because they cannot afford, being Day Schools, to have games in the afternoons. They are bound to work for about two hours in the afternoon for at least four days in the week, and more often five. The Public Schools can work after tea and do prep. in the evening, so that they can afford to be out of doors every afternoon.

The cumulative effect of this on physical vigour is tremendous.

Psychologically, on the other hand, the Secondary Schools score by being Day Schools. Monday morning at a Secondary School is (in my experience) a cheerful time. Pupils and staff, not having seen each other since Friday afternoon, if they are lucky, or Saturday morning, if they are not, are quite glad to meet each other. (They may have met at the Saturday afternoon match, but that was fun.) It is often a minor difficulty at a Secondary School that the children come on to the school premises at an incredibly early hour. Monday morning at a Public School, specially in the second half of the term, is a depressing spectacle; almost more depressing in the common-room that in the class rooms. Everyone has lived in close contact with everyone else till they feel like murder. Sunday has only offered enough change to make one realize one's condition. For three months there is no escape from one's pet enemy. It is said that, when parties of explorers are made up, the first care of the leader is to see that no-one in the party will get on anyone else's nerves. Any boy or master (and still more, any girl or mistress) at a Public School can believe this easily. It sounds funny, but it isn't.

The physical defects of the Secondary Schools and the psychological defects of the Public Schools are most serious. A child is not good for much if he is ill or ill-adjusted.

8. *Progressive Schools with an Idea Behind Them.*

There are two sorts of Progressive Schools, those with an idea, and those that really believe in freedom for children.

They are sometimes muddled up with each other, but they are really quite different. Those with an idea want to mould their children to it, and in this resemble the Public Schools (though the idea is quite different from the Public School idea). The free progressive schools have despaired of our civilization, and think that if we start again from scratch we may be all right. They hold the dogma of the fundamental goodness of children, and believe that we only need let it operate.

The Progressive Schools with an idea are above all well-meaning. They are commonly generous and affectionate, and have intelligent teachers and parents, but probably not the most intelligent children. The Public Schools and the efficient Secondary Schools are so much more skilful at getting University Entrance Scholarships, and the value of these Scholarships is so immense, that the parents of really brilliant children (particularly boys, since practically all the University scholarships are for boys) tend to send them to the schools which are most likely to get these scholarships.

But Progressive Schools with an idea have most serious disadvantages.

They attract cranks. Cranks are often people who have externalized an internal conflict without understanding it. For this reason they are rightly suspected People who feel something seriously wrong may externalize it and blame the world. Then they try to reform the world because this is less personally uncomfortable than trying to reform themselves. Hence Bentham's remark: "Reformers are necessary, but the practice of their trade makes them unsavoury." It need not if they reform themselves as well as other things. There is plenty of scope both within and without.

People who have externalized a conflict are sometimes really devastating, especially to children. They are the worst of all oppressors, for they see everyone else as actors on a stage in a play whose theme is their own personal conflict. Without knowing it, they may try to make children take the appropriate parts in this play.

These schools, therefore, make the Public School mistake of knowing what they want and getting it, and so preventing the world from growing any better. Educationally, this is one of the worst of all mistakes. Our only hope is that our children should find out things that are beyond our range. Any mould that we can imagine is within our range.

These schools also provoke another of the worst disasters—the laying of a veneer of good behaviour, moral fervour, and uplift on top of the real person, and so ultimately producing a hopelessly divided personality.

All preaching to those who cannot escape it is an abomination, and exhortation in private (unless it is asked for by the exhorted) is worse. It is an evasion and a covering up of the real situation.

There was until recently a progressive Public School which had a system called the Honour System, which gives a fine example of the very worst way of governing a school. It is described as follows by someone who had experienced it:—

"About a week after arrival every new boy was interviewed separately by his Housemaster and the Headmaster, and was asked—I need hardly say how difficult it would have been to refuse—to promise on his honour three things:

(1) Not to swear,
(2) Not to smoke,
(3) Not to say or do anything indecent.

Having done so, two consequences followed:

(1) If you broke any of these promises you should report the breakage to your housemaster.
(2) If you saw anyone else break them, you should endeavour to persuade him to report, and if he refused, you should report him yourself.

Before I say anything in criticism, I must add that the system worked, in public at any rate. One almost never saw anyone smoke, heard anyone swear, or came across any smut. From the point of view of master and parent it would seem ideal.

From the boys' point of view, on the other hand,

I feel compelled to say that no more potent engine for turning them into neurotic innocents, for perpetuating those faults of character it was intended to cure was ever devised."[1]

This is an attack on the essential freedom of the spirit. At a normal Public School one is at least free to break the rules and take the consequences, but the Honour System is a spiritual imprisonment.

The Progressive Schools with an idea do not do exactly this; but the spirit of it is akin to theirs. The slavery to someone else's idea may assail and capture the central citadel of the spirit. Moral oppression, if it succeeds, is worse than physical oppression.

Preaching at a Public School is formal, and is rarely taken seriously. Private exhortation is called a "pi-jaw" (or it used to be, for probably there are better and more striking names now) and is suffered with fortitude and ignored. One knows the poor fellow has to do it. ("My God, I've got to do sixteen Confirmation candidates this week," as the Housemaster at a Public School may be heard to say.)

But preaching and exhortation are far more dangerous where there is no corporal punishment to make fools of them by showing up their insincerity. They may "take" and reduce the school to the condition of a field that has been smothered in artificial manure.

9. *Progressive Free Schools.*

The disadvantage of the Progressive Free Schools

[1] This, with most valuable comments following it, is in "The Old School," edited by Graham Greene. (Jonathan Cape.)

is that Liberalism is not enough. Humanity has landed itself in a mess, and whatever the cause of this mess may be we can be sure that it is inside us. Not without reason have the churches insisted on the doctrine of original sin. There is something within us which is not to be trusted. I regret that it is called "original sin," because the idea of sin is associated with that unprofitable exercise of the spirit—moral disapproval. I think it would be better to call it "muddle," as I suggested at the beginning of this essay, but there is certainly something which puts us wrong.

There is, I think, rather a danger that the Progressive Free Schools may have cranks on their staff, that the children may remain for too long remote and cushioned from the world they will have to live in, and that the staff may really only want to do nothing and avoid responsibility; but none of these faults is really of the first magnitude.

These schools give us, at least, a chance of learning what to do by trial and error, a long and expensive but not hopeless method. But there are very few of them as yet.

I think they are wrong in supposing that children are all right if left to themselves; and this seems to me such a serious error that I should feel very uncomfortable if a child of my own were at a Progressive Free School. In fact, children can't be left to themselves at any school, however free. They are bound to be affected by the character of the adults, and by the general feeling of the place. It is better for adults to recognize this, accept the responsibility, and not

257

label the school "free." I should very much like to be
on the staff myself—for a time at least—to see what
really happened.

I am inclined to class the Free Progressive Schools
as the most hopeful, in spite of their obvious disadvantages, provided that they really stick to their
present habits of absolute truthfulness. They are the
only schools, and quite possibly the only institutions,
where what is said and done really correspond to what
is felt. I see a unity of speech, action, and feeling as a
way of life, and a policy of putting a good face on
things as a way of death.

These schools are too few to do much directly as yet.
But what they discover, if they maintain their honesty
and friendliness, may in time affect the mass of schools.

The special characteristics of schoolmasters and
schoolmistresses, as such, are part of the problem.

Almost every schoolmaster regards it as the highest
sincere compliment he can be paid when he is mistaken
for something else.

If you are told that a stranger you are just going to
meet is a schoolmaster or schoolmistress, you have a
momentary shiver of horror. (I have heard that Lord
Roberts felt the same about cats.) If, after the meeting,
you detect signs of humanity, you are agreeably sur-
prised.

Everyone who has served on a school staff knows that
tight-rope feeling; that feeling that if you say or do a
single thing which is wrong by a hair's breadth there
will be a crash. I remember once at the Annual

Meeting of the Science Masters Association, a most valuable body of which I am very glad to be a member, I went to a lecture. I was a little late and most of the audience was there.

As I opened the door an inner voice spoke to me, quite without warning, saying: *"There are more than 150 schoolmasters in that room; escape while you can."* I did so, though I think science-masters and geography-masters have it much less badly than other kinds, being often scientists and geographers as well.

Now let us see what it was I recoiled from. We must isolate the schoolmaster-horror from the crowd-horror.

Imagine yourself on the threshold of a room containing 150 people, packed fairly close but not unhygienically close. Picture to yourself your feelings if you knew the room contained:

- (*a*) School-teachers
- (*b*) Parsons
- (*c*) Butchers
- (*d*) Huntin' and shootin' county people
- (*e*) Teaching-dons
- (*f*) Research-dons
- (*g*) Doctors in General Practice
- (*h*) Harley Street doctors
- (*i*) Railway porters
- (*j*) Railway signalmen
- (*k*) Ordinary soldiers or sailors
- (*l*) Generals and Admirals
- (*m*) Headmasters and Headmistresses
- (*n*) Hedgers and ditchers

- (*o*)   Cowmen
- (*p*)   Country innkeepers
- (*q*)   Town innkeepers
- (*r*)   Members of the House of Commons
- (*s*)   Members of the House of Lords
- (*t*)   Technical experts of electrical firms
- (*u*)   Successful novelists
- (*v*)   Unsuccessful novelists
- (*w*)   Oxford Groupers
- (*x*)   Revivalist preachers
- (*y*)   London 'bus-drivers and conductors
- (*z*)   Actors and actresses

I do not know how the reader will feel about this list. From my experience I unhesitatingly pick porters, signalmen, hedgers and ditchers, cowmen and London 'busmen as the best; and I should put research-dons, doctors in general practice, and technical experts next, and inferior only because they are in danger of intellectual pride. In all these occupations humbug will not wash (except for a little conscious humbug in doctors). None find it their duty to try and improve other people's morals or characters. All have either frequent and warm-hearted contact with all sorts and conditions of men, or else frequent opportunities for contemplation.

In some of the professions on the list people feel themselves responsible for the morals of others, give moral advice when it is not asked for, take consciously moral attitudes, set good examples on purpose, or pretend to feel what they don't feel.

All professions which require these things tend to corrupt the character, and of such professions that of teaching is in the highest grade.

Serious people who deceive themselves by their own pretensions are corrupted far more than people who, like doctors prescribing tonics, deceive others but not themselves.

This line of thought suggests, too, that a good education should be founded on three main things: the habit of truthfulness even when it is most inconvenient (particularly the true expression of feelings), warm-hearted contact with all sorts of people, and opportunities for contemplation alone. It also suggests that teaching should be scheduled high in the list of dangerous trades.

There is one most important thing not always realized about teachers. They must have lives of their own, independent of the life of the school. This fact alone ensures that almost all married men teachers in Day-Schools with happy family lives (so adjusted that they neither turn to school as a relief from home nor to home as a relief from school) are good teachers, and centres of life for their pupils.

A Day-School teacher has a much better chance of a life of his own than one in a boarding-school. But Day-Schools can be completely absorbing especially to unmarried teachers; all of whom should certainly have strong non-school connexions in the district.

Moreover, whole-hearted devotees (especially to causes involving a direct personal effect on others) though sometimes extremely useful, are on the whole dangerous to society by being at once powerful and irresponsible through lack of a sense of proportion.

The schools I have written about include among them both Boarding- and Day-Schools. I do not feel that the discussion of the rather obvious advantages and disadvantages of these two types is relevant to this essay. The Secondary Schools and the progressive schools also include among them both mixed (or co-educational) schools and single-sex schools. The arguments for and against mixed schools are partly obvious and partly obscure. I doubt if the position will become really clear until the higher education of women has been ordinary, rather than exceptional, for a very long time.

There are several more educational problems of first-rate importance which I have not discussed; as, for example, homework in Secondary Schools, what the curriculum ought to be to equip children for ordinary needs of life (as they certainly are not equipped now), examinations and their effects, and the problem of getting children to know all they certainly should know about both their bodies and their minds. They learn almost nothing now in most schools about bodies or minds. I should like to tackle all of them, and more; but, as with the problems of mixed and single-sex schools, and of Boarding- and Day-Schools, I do not feel they are relevant to this essay. I am not quite sure about this, but the differences of view about them seem to me straightforward differences with, so to speak, the devil not taking a hand in the game. (In schools which know what type they want to produce, and produce it, and in wrong treatment of infants, the devil does take a hand.)

I think straightforward debate will clear these problems up in time, and if the heart were right they would come right. But if they were put right, they would not put the heart right; and putting the heart right, finding some general line of attack for everyone concerned, whatever sides they take in all the controversy, is what I am after in this essay.

I have one more point about schools. I am very much inclined to think that large schools are wrong because they tend to become institutional and inhuman. I suspect that everyone in a school, including children and staff, should know everyone else well as a person, because this allows development of sensitiveness to other people's feelings. No school should be too large for this to be possible. For this reason I fear the Hadow reorganization scheme may do much harm by inducing the local authorities to do away with the small village school and send the village children to the larger junior or senior school in the nearest centre; by making the village conform to a scheme which is obviously valuable in towns (making everything conform to a theory for the sake of principle) much that is valuable and irreplacable may be lost. The bigger schools may be more institutional, more inhuman, and though far more efficient in the purely intellectual part of the teaching may lose more than they gain in the growth of the human spirit.

If Dr. Edward Glover is right about the education we shall need in the future in what he calls his Utopia, then the small village schools are the nearest to what we should have for everyone. "If there are still city streets in Utopia, then every fourth house in those streets will be a school for children between the ages of four and seven, with a maximum of ten children and staff of four, of whom two will themselves be children about the age of puberty. For Utopia will involve the restoration of child labour to a place of dignity in social life. I need hardly add that these schools will not be prisons and that they will not be compulsory. Specialising will still have its place in education but for children from seven to puberty the central school will be reduced to the status of a half-time institution.

"Small special schools of all sorts will be everywhere, just as shops are everywhere at present. Children will be able to pick up their education with the same freedom that good housekeepers go marketing. They will be taught to play and learn just as present-day adults do; that is to say, in their own way and their own time. At puberty education can with safety become centralized and systematized—for the emancipated adolescent will learn what is necessary with rapidity."[1] The small village schools are not like what this suggests. But they are much less unlike it than any other sorts. We may need them later, so it is a pity to lose them now.

In my survey of the schools I have been trying to note things that are outstandingly valuable or outstandingly disastrous. I do not think there is anything outstandingly valuable or disastrous about a Boarding-School as

[1] "The Dangers of Being Human". Dr. Edward Glover; and *Listener*.

such, a Day-School as such, a mixed school as such, or a single-sex school as such. But I suggest that the fairly obvious psychological disadvantage of Boarding-Schools and single-sex schools will tend to make mixed Day-Schools increasingly important.

VI

THE ROOT OF THE MATTER

What are we to do about all this?

If you are ill, the trouble may come from inside you, or from outside you, or from both. It may be because you are unhappy, or it may be because you live in a slum. The cure probably needs alteration of both yourself and the slum. To alter one would not be enough.

To cure our educational diseases we must both alter conditions and alter ourselves.

I want to tackle the problem of the cure without being controversial. We can find quite enough to get on with in what is self-evident. I begin with those alterations to external conditions which seem to me both obvious and possible within the existing structure of society. Most of them can be done quickly if the local authorities have the will to do them.

1. All educational authorities should do their utmost with the help of recommendations from the County Medical Authority if necessary, to see that no children in their area suffer from malnutrition. This is the first job for educators. If the children cannot be properly fed at home, they must be fed at school. Moreover, they must be given well-balanced and well-cooked

266

meals; not the casual and miscellaneous fill-ups they get at many schools now. Every area needs a diet expert to see that school meals are the right sort.

This feeding of children would only touch the fringe of the problem of poverty, unemployment and malnutrition. But if only a few can be saved it is to the interest of the community that the children should be saved first.

With the present economic background, all education, and particularly all luxury education, has a strong suggestion of farce about it. To see that the children being educated are adequately fed would make it less farcical.

2. There should be enough Nursery Schools throughout the country for all the small children that need them, instead of only a few here and there. The establishment of Nursery Schools throughout England would make more difference to the character of the adult generation of thirty years hence than any other single possible change.

3. In a recently published County Annual Report on Education there was a note of regret and apology because the number of teachers in the county had not yet been reduced, although the number of children in the schools had fallen. There was also what appeared to be a promise of "amendment," a promise to reduce the number of teachers in future so that the numbers of children per teacher in the county should remain constant.

This attitude is most dangerous. The number of teachers in Elementary and Secondary Schools is just about half what it should be. Classes are at least twice as large as they should be.

If the child-population of the country fell to about half its present level, and the number of teachers and accommodation in school buildings remained as it is now, the proportions would be about right.

So long as this fact is evaded, or not recognized, by competent authorities, education will remain what it is now—a standardizing, stultifying, mass-producing process, instead of the living business it might be if the staffing were enough to allow habitual personal individual contact, and discussion rather than instruction.

4. The health and happiness of nursing mothers particularly from nine months before birth to two years after should be put in the very centre of all problems tackled by all Governments. It has never been so yet.

5. There should be child-guidance clinics available for every school in every area, to be used for those apparently minor behaviour problems and social aberations which, untreated, or treated according to the ordinary routine of (frequently repressive) discipline, develop into serious defects of character in later life.

At present, there are very few of these clinics; and those available are compelled by pressure of work to give their attention mainly to very serious cases; though actually the "slight" cases are just as serious, and repay treatment much more fully.

6. There should be a modification of the policy of the Hadow Report, by which there is gradually developing throughout the country a separation between schools for children under eleven and for those

over eleven. This form of reorganization works well in towns, but it is very dangerous in the country, for it means first decapitation (removal of senior children) and later abolition of the small village schools. This is thoroughly bad for two main reasons:

(*a*) The close personal contact between teacher, children and parents in a small village school is one of the best forges of character possible, if the teacher is a sympathetic person. It produces a combination of independence, friendliness and social responsibility which is much less common in large schools;

(*b*) With the roads as dangerous as they are now and will probably continue to be, parents hate to send their children to school to another village. Young married couples, therefore, avoid settling in a village without a school. The Hadow reorganization scheme, if it is fully carried out in the rural districts, will therefore mean the gradual death of most of the villages, because parents with young children will not stay in them. The death of the villages will mean the deterioration—the continued deterioration, for it has already begun—of farming and rural life generally through shortage of labour; and from the point of view of the country at large this will be a bad change.

I realize that the small village school cannot show the variety of teachers or knowledge that is possible in a large school formed by combining several village schools, but I think that the importance of knowledge, as it can be got from books and from academic teachers, has been very much exaggerated. The character that can be formed in school is very much more important than the knowledge that can be gained. It is much easier to pick up knowledge in later life, if one wants it, than to alter radically a character that has set wrong in early years.

I know that the Public Schools consider themselves primarily as formers of characters. It seems to me that they really are good at giving knowledge without character. Their knowledge is head-knowledge, and they only touch the heart to standardize it. The character formed by Public Schools or large schools is too mass-produced, standardized, insensitive, either repressive or repressed, and, in those naturally sensitive, too neurotic.

The small schools, the schools so small that everyone knows everyone, and each individual counts, tend to produce characters socially responsible, friendly, sympathetic, independent-thinking, and stable.

7. The school life of the average child at a secondary School is bounded at both ends by examinations. At the age of eleven the child passes in through the door of the special Place Scholarship Examination, and at the age of sixteen meets the School Certificate Examination.

Both, though extremely convenient from the point of view of educational organizers, have a bad effect on the children by standardizing the curriculum and putting a premium on the appearance to understand, rather than on actual understanding, in school work. The aim of the school becomes to teach the "right" subjects and make the children give the "right" answers to questions on these subjects.

All I can urge here is that the study and reform of both these examinations should be pressed on with real energy, with the final idea of alterations to them so complete as to be equivalent to their abolition; or at least the abolition of the factors in them that lead to standardization and the divorce of learning from living.

I suggest as an immediate step in the right direction that the special place examination should depend on the school record and on Intelligence tests, instead of on examination results in formal English and Arithmetic. Local authorities should encourage the keeping of thorough school records, and call in psychologists to help in research in this problem, as some authorities do now; and they should use as much as possible the very valuable mass of work that has been done on the testing of intelligence.

I suggest that the very arbitrary division between passing and failing in the School Certificate should be abolished. It is possible to pass with one credit and fail with five, and all the University Examinations Boards suffer severe biennial headaches in the hopeless attempt to be fair in separating the sheep from the goats. Those who want to take the examination could take it, and get from the University a certified record of what they had done in each subject taken. This change would be far from making the examination satisfactory, but it would cut off the worst of the fetters which are now preventing reasonable evolution and would do so without causing any severe disturbance in the existing scheme.

8. I hesitate to make my last recommendation, but I feel it is so important that it cannot be avoided. Much of the work of educational organization in districts outside the big towns falls on the well-off people of the district, largely on the country gentleman, clergymen, and retired or prosperous business men, and of course their wives. They serve as managers, school governors, and on Education Committees. Most of them generously give up time and energy to this work; but their general attitude to it is bound to be much too detached while their own children are at Public Schools, and are therefore immune to the consequences of their parent's educational decisions, though I have no doubt that they would be much less easily satisfied with building, staffing, and educational opportunities than they now are, if their own children were involved.

If a majority of the country gentlemen, and the well-off people generally, could be induced to send their children to the Elementary and Secondary Schools, both the buildings and the staffing of many of these schools would be improved out of all recognition in the twinkling of an eye.

I cannot call for this reform with any serious hope that it will come about, for one of the strongest of human desires is to give one's own children the best chance, quite regardless of other people's. Practically all well-off people are sure that the best chance for their children is in the Public Schools.

All I can call for is that the well-off will make a much more serious attempt to imagine their own children at the schools they administer, and that they will realize that though their own children are safe at well-to-do schools, taxation and the breaking-up of estates may force their grandchildren to the ordinary schools.

It may really genuinely be worth their while to get the elementary and secondary schools good enough for themselves instead of being merely good enough for those others.

I think myself that the basic difficulty here may be almost a theological one.

The Christian belief in the equality of souls before God has rarely been taken seriously in England except at the time of death. People dying are generally regarded as important in their own right, but hardly people living.

That ends my recommendation for the altering of external conditions—not because I have finished, but because I have said enough to go on with—and I turn to the altering of things within ourselves. The progressive alteration of individuals is the root of the matter Again I want to avoid controversy, for it wastes our energies by splitting us into opposing camps yet again.

I suggest that we were given the root of the matter a pretty long time ago, and that we have not yet begun to take any serious notice of it. It is that we as individuals must first alter ourselves and then see what we do .

Now we try to find the right thing to do, and hope that doing it will alter ourselves, or that if we do the right things it won't matter what we are really like. Both these hopes are illusory.

"The Kingdom of Heaven is within you."
"Seek ye first the Kingdom of God and
His righteousness, and all these things
shall be added unto you."

This is the clue. But it has never yet been followed up, except by rare individuals. George Fox, the first Quaker, was once consulted by another Quaker who felt uncomfortable about wearing a sword according to the custom for gentlemen at the time. Although it was only part of a dress, he felt that it symbolized something inconsistent with Quakerism. He asked what he should do about it.

"Wear it as long as thou canst," said George Fox.

This is universal. If you are doubtful about the rightness of something, "wear it as long as thou canst." When you can no longer wear it, you will have changed. and in that respect will be trustworthy, because the change will be from within, and not a top dressing.

This care for appearances, with indifference to what lies behind, is near the heart of all our educational problems. Edmond Holmes has brought it out very clearly in his book "What is and What might be." I have seen it explained as an unexpected result of the Calvinistic doctrine of election. According to this doctrine, a few are predestined by God to salvation, and what they actually do does not affect their ultimate fate. The rest are predestined to damnation. One would naturally suppose that people who believed this would not bother about trying to be good at all. But actually the doctrine had a very different effect. It was believed that the elect would not be able to help being good, and people therefore tried to convince both others and themselves, by their outward and visible behaviour, that they were of the elect. The whole emphasis was therefore thrown on an appearance of goodness; and it remains there to this day, especially in schools (except the Free Progressive Schools). This insistence on the importance of outward behaviour, and on what makes a show, has had two principal effects in schools to-day. It shows in the present importance of marks and orders, and on the passing of exams. rather than the understanding of the subject. People tend to want a first-class degree in History rather than to be historians; to get a piece of paper as evidence that they have passed the School Certificate and "studied" all the things enumerated in the "Course of Study" written on the back; to be top of the form and have that fact clearly stated on reports.

This effect, though damaging, is not so damaging as the other, which I will try to explain, although it is rather hard to explain it clearly.

Children who are happy in themselves do on the whole behave well. If their parents and teachers are worthy of respect they get treated with respect. All this is desirable, and is the outward and visible sign of an inward and spiritual state of children, parents, and teachers. It is a state we all want. But parents and teachers think that if they compel children to behave as they would if all were well, this behaviour will gradually induce the appropriate feelings within; and also produce evidence that they (the teachers and parents) are as they should be.

This idea is a dangerous illusion. It simply makes the recovery of an ill-adjusted child more difficult, or sometimes impossible.

Headmasters, in particular, are expected to go all out for good behaviour, using dangerous means towards this desirable end if necessary. I am not in the least saying that the law should be abrogated. The perfect motorist would not drive to the public danger. If a motorist does drive to the public danger it may be due to faults which would not have developed in him if his parents had had more sense. In a way, therefore, he is unlucky if he is punished. He must be punished by the community to make it not worth while for him to be a public danger. The punishment will not reform him, though it may deter him. He ought to be reformed as well (a slow job). I am not in the least saying that schools should have no law and order; but I am trying to make it clear that many schools now insist on "good" behaviour direct, with the idea that it will improve character. It is like insisting that a sick man must walk ten miles a day because he might do so naturally if he were healthy.

I do not know enough history to be sure if I am right in supposing this widespread regard for outward evidence of internal goodness, without any regard for internal goodness, grew out of the Calvinistic doctrine of predestination to salvation or damnation. Probably Calvinism gave more scope to a deep-seated desire in all humanity to pretend that all is well and suppress symptoms. When you have a stomach-ache you try to get an immediate cure out of the doctor, and do not think about the real cause; for removing the real cause may mean altering your whole way of life.

The first step towards the cure of this general evil is to understand; and for this reason I try to state it.

When people are changed by preaching, the change is from without, is a top dressing, and is not to be trusted.

By being changed I do not mean what the Oxford Groups mean (though I approve their insistence that the individual must change first, and see what he does afterwards, rather than tackle institutions directly).

The changing by the Groups is from outside, by exhortation and mass-suggestion.

The sort of changing that works is a slower, more painful (and sometimes more expensive) business.

For the few people who can afford the time and money, change and development may come through a course of psycho-analysis, but we cannot rely on this for several reasons, of which the first is that it is too expensive, and the second that it may become a game or a craze, and may be continued for its own sake. But its method of self-knowledge without moral condemnation, and the gradual exploration of feelings that have sunk below the surface of consciousness, but continue to operate there, is the right sort of method.

Here again we have had the clues, but have not followed them up.

"Resist not evil."

"Judge not."

"Resist not evil" is very far from meaning "Do

nothing about evil." It means that we should understand and get behind something we see to be evil,
rather than oppose it directly. In particular, we must
understand evil in ourselves, rather than saying: "I
will put this out of my mind."

Putting a thing out of one's mind does not cure the
evil, but it does disunite the personality, and it makes
very sure of keeping the evil in one's mind, but below
the surface of consciousness, where it can do most
harm.

Most of the things that happen in the mind must be
below the surface of consciousness. That is all right.
There is no need to drag them up unless they are at
war. But when they are at war they must be dragged
up and sorted out.

"Judge not" is almost the same thing. It is short for
"Do not waste your time in moral condemnations."
When you want to condemn morally, try to find out the
true cause instead. Your energy will be well-spent so,
instead of ill-spent.

I think I can illustrate the necessity of changing
oneself and then seeing what one does, rather than
trying to make sure of doing the right thing direct.

A healthy man likes to use his mind and his body. He
runs and thinks and is happy.

A sick man may want to sit about and do nothing
with either his body or his mind. The doctor knows
that the sick man ought to behave as the healthy one
does, but that "ought" does not mean that he should
be made to do it directly. It means that his behaviour
is an indication that he is unhealthy. If the doctor

makes the sick man run at once, he may kill instead of curing.

The quickest (and indeed only) way to get the sick man to do what he should is to make him healthy. Then he will do the right things naturally. Most of our schools, and the people in them, are like the sick man. One can see at a glance that there are hideous things wrong with most of them.

But it is the wrong method to work out what schools should do, and make our schools do them. We, both educators and educated, must change ourselves and then see what we do. There is nothing at all dramatic about this.

> *"And bravery is now*
> *Not in the dying breath,*
> *But resisting the temptations*
> *To skyline operations."*[1]

It is most important to realize that the process of self-changing or continuous self-development is not a matter of the conscious will. To make good resolutions, except about quite minor and exclusively personal matters, only makes one worse.

To have a cold bath every morning is good for some people, but not important. To feel really friendly to others is most important. But to resolve to have a cold bath every morning may be quite a good thing, whereas to resolve to feel friendly towards someone who hitherto has always infuriated you, by the effort of your con-

[1]W. H. Auden. Poems. (Faber & Faber.)

19

scious will, might put you at war with yourself and incidentally make you intolerable to everyone else.

To want to "love your enemies" is all right; but the way to do it (if it can be done) is to find out about the situation. If the origin of the trouble is in yourself, you will change yourself in the process of finding out. If the trouble is outside yourself you will be able to handle it better if you understand it. But you must ask yourself questions and give yourself true answers, without passing judgment or morally condemning.

At the end of this essay I will put a list of suggestions about changing and developing oneself fundamentally. Most of the instructions, by the way, appear to have been given by Jesus nearly 2,000 years ago, very tersely and cryptically.

But most people have heard them said so often and so reverently that now they can be pretty well unaffected by them. The familiar words touch a spring which shuts a door in the mind and keeps their meaning outside, where it can cause no discomfort.

I fear all this solution I offer may seem to give nothing definite to catch hold of. I can make one definite suggestion, and only one.

The more an individual can get rid of fear, greed and malice, the better (and incidentally the more of a power) he is. Fear includes anxiety about dignity or prestige. Greed includes all ambition, and particularly the desire for power; malice includes the absence of a friendly attitude to the world. Now it is almost impossible to be in any sort of authority and be clear of fear, greed and malice in these senses. Every teacher, and particularly every headmaster and headmistress, would do well to keep in close touch with whoever of those available is nearest to being clear of fear, greed, and malice. The adviser would be disqualified by occupying a position of authority; or by being so situated that he might be injured in self-respect, reputation, or anything else, by a failure of his consultant. People like this are too rare for everybody in authority to be able to find one. But I think all should try.

There is a Chinese saying: "First secure an independent income; and then practise the virtues."

Consider also Lord Acton's remark: "Power always corrupts; absolute power absolutely corrupts."

Unfortunately, the headmasters, who hold the key positions, are usually compelled by the nature of their jobs to change in the wrong direction, if at all.

Who would willingly go into a room if he knew it contained five headmasters? Headmasters are compelled to watch rather than do, to be rushed off their feet with business, to say what they don't mean and leave unsaid what they do mean till eventually they cannot really mean anything at all. Continually they judge, and resist evil. They spend their lives fetching the motes out of other people's eyes, and have little time for the operation which should come before this. (Another long-neglected clue here, by the way.)

"Blessed are the meek, for they shall inherit the earth." (Another neglected clue.) The meek are the adaptable, the people who are not too proud to adjust themselves to circumstances, who are not afraid to admit they have been wrong.

To refuse, or be unable, to adapt oneself is the way of death, and many headmasters there are that find it. I who write am a headmaster for the second time. The other day someone at a school I was visiting said to me: "What is the biggest obstacle in the way of getting your school to be as it ought to be?" I had a moment of insight and said: "I am." It was true, and it is true for all of us. Nevertheless it is but a small part of the truth. I was putting too high a value on myself. For many factors independent of the Headmaster operate against every school.

VII

GERALD HEARD'S book, *The Source of Civilization*, gives evidence that sensitiveness and the power to undertake fundamental change are the survival factors in evolution, and that efficiency and adaptation to environment lead to extinction when ultimately environment changes, as it must. He therefore advocates the continual deep-seated change and development of individuals in the direction of greatest sensitiveness as our right path.

Note the story of Nicodemus (about the only intellectual Jesus encountered) in the 3rd Chapter of St. John's Gospel. Note that Jesus answers in Verse 3 the question that Nicodemus did not ask in Verse 2, and when Nicodemus asks for an explanation in Verse 4, Jesus does not even try to give one, but simply repeats what He said. He leaves Nicodemus to find out how to do it. Annoying, but the only way.

Do not be afraid of affection towards or from anyone whatever.

Do not be afraid of giving yourself away, or of looking a fool. You are one. So is everyone else.

Most people's real feelings have been "put wrong" by their lives, especially their early lives. This damage could be repaired if unconscious growth and change were continuous, for the fool who persisted in his folly would become wise.

But most people are fixated (or, if you prefer it, fixed) pretty young, because growth and change are painful and troublesome, and to stay put is the line of least resistance. Continuous change and growth are necessary for all individuals, in the sense that those who have lost the power of growth and change are equivalent to cancers in the community; organizing, consuming, and functioning independently.

Yet no one can change himself, or restart the process of growth once stopped, by a direct effort of the will. The will can direct actions but not feelings, and it is feelings which count here. Good resolutions are bad. But the problem is not so hopeless as it sounds.

There are methods of circumventing the will, and of using it profitably. For example, if one puts oneself into unfamiliar surroundings or situations, and cuts off retreat so that one has to live into them, it may be useful.

One can will oneself into a state of receptivity rather than a state of refusal, and wait to see what comes; one can, for example, gradually build up the habit of paying serious attention to what other people say, instead of living one's life as an endless visit to the human Zoo. One can take enough trouble over health to avoid being incapacitated by constipation, oxygen-lack, vitamin-deficiency, or mineral-salt deficiency. This is particularly important for teachers. They get content with a low standard of health, and gradually get more helpless, more hopeless, and worse-tempered as the years go on, without ever getting quite bad enough to die or retire.

This is specially true of middle-aged teachers. They are kept indoors on most afternoons by school work; they take no exercise; and they eat devitalized food at home or in lodgings; so that when they get stuck in a rut they simply have not the guts to do anything but stay in it and hate mankind. When their constipation is noticeably worse than usual, they take a strong aperient and start again, like a dishonest business man making terms with his conscience by going to church on Sunday. But the human digestive organs are astonishingly long-suffering. You can ill-treat them till you are fifty, and then get them in very fair order by beginning to eat sensible food and live a reasonable life.

If what you seem to other people is different from what you are, it is better to seem stupider or worse than you are than wiser or better.

To be expected to feel gratitude or give applause is an abomination; so do not look for them from others. It is all right if you get them by accident.

Beware of the parsonical, political, or magisterial voice in yourself or others—specially in reading prayers, if you have to. They are evidence of simulated emotion.

You may have to behave as if you were better than you are to avoid immediate catastrophe. But it is dangerous, all the same.

When you spot something wrong, either in yourself or elsewhere, do not be excited or appalled, but try to find out the real cause, without passing judgment, before you act, if the pressure of circumstances allows you to avoid immediate action.

Keep time for contemplation at all costs.

Never try to impress your philosophy on anyone else.

Do not be *unco guid*. (It is risky to be a teetotaller on principle.)

> *"So our goody-good men betray us*
> *And our sainty-saints let us down."*[1]

Do not think out your plan of action too far ahead, but consider the lilies and follow your nose. From his book, *The Faith of a Schoolmaster* I suspect that Sharwood Smith did this, and it seems to have worked. He does it still in 1937.

Do not set a good example on purpose. It is harmless, and may even be useful, if you don't know you are doing it.

Do not worry whether your feelings are appropriate. And on no account pretend to yourself that they are what they are not. The worst mistake of all about feelings is to be intimidated by anyone else into having what seem to be the right ones.

Changing yourself does not mean one big change and all's well. It is a continuous process until death. Best of all, if it goes on till the death of the body. But anyway, when change stops death has come. Many corpses still hold the office of headmaster.

[1] D. H. Lawrence. (Heinemann.)

Be quite literally truthful as often as you possibly can, unless you can see that truth-telling will lead to immediate disaster. (But don't be free with inconvenient or unpleasant truths about other people. Your motive may not be what you think. Judge not.)

Do not go all moral about other people, (especially children,) who tell lies. They may have very good reasons for telling lies. In fact, lies may be their only method of defence against dangers they ought not to have encountered. But if you find people (especially children) telling lies, try to find out the real reason for it without asking awkward questions, or, still worse, *de haut en bas* questions.

Beware of theorists, idealists, people who make it sound as if everything is lovely in the garden, and people who know exactly what to do.

Understanding the Child, published at 1s. by the Home and School Council, 29 Tavistock Square, London, W.C.1., is not only about schoolchildren, but is equally about anyone sensible enough to learn.

Do not be in a hurry to give good advice except to avoid imminent disaster. It is all right to give it if you are genuinely and spontaneously asked for it.

"Take no thought how or what ye shall speak; for it shall be given you in that same hour what ye shall speak."

Never get into an argument or discussion without realizing that you may have something to learn, and being willing to be convinced; for it is no good discussing anything with an opponent who cannot, or dare not change his mind; and (specially in dealing with children) you must never be such an opponent.

(Headmasters who send for boys to tell them off frequently know exactly what they will say, and simply dare not be proved wrong. The boy realizes, and politely ignores such people.)

Having your mind changed about something which really matters will probably be just what you need.

"Speak what we feel not what we ought to say."

Children deeply need contact with unprejudiced adults; and the demand for them very much exceeds the supply.

"In a world dominated by monsters, the future is given to a creature which has to spend its time taking notice of others and giving way to others."

This was written about the geological age of the dinosaurs, perhaps fifty million years ago. It was not intended as a description of a school, but it is one. Guess the identity of the monsters.

It is all right to blame in the sense that, if you think Tommy caught his cold from George, you blame George, or in the sense that if you think Tommy caught his cold by getting his feet wet, you might blame Tommy for not having more sense, or his mother for letting him get like that.

The cure is to isolate George (but if George is a well-established schoolteacher this takes some doing), or get better shoes, or let Tommy have more practice in looking after himself. In the meantime the cold must run its course.

It is even worse to blame yourself morally. You

must, without moral condemnation, find out the truth about yourself.

Both about other people and about yourself be an anthropologist who is not afraid to feel.

V

RELIGION

H. R. L. Sheppard

RELIGION

THE Concise Oxford Dictionary says that religion is "human recognition of super-human controlling power . . . effect of such recognition on conduct and mental attitude," and that is not so bad for a dictionary. It gives the derivation of the word, too, from the Latin *religare*, to bind. A religious man, then, is bound to God. But he is also bound together in himself, he is integrated, he is whole. Bound to God, he knows God for part of himself and himself for part of God, and knows that he is made in God's image. Whole within himself, and bound to God, the religious man is the sane man, perhaps the only sane man in an insane world; for "the sane man is the whole man, and the whole man is God."

But there are so many different ways of being a religious man, and so many different sorts of religious man. As the centuries have passed, religion seems to have lost its quality of being a "binding," and to have become very often the opposite, a separation. Followers of one sect, though they follow the same teacher as another sect, are divided against and separated from the followers of that other : it is not only that the followers of Christ look upon the followers of Buddha as heathens. The followers of the Pope, who follow Christ, look upon the followers of Wesley, who follow

Christ, as something very like heathens. The churches have raised their own dogmas, with the passing of the years, to a position of as great importance in their histories and in the lives of their adherents as the teaching of their Founder: sometimes even to greater importance, so that it is forgotten that we are all one in Christ. Yet in all these many religions, these many sects of each religion, there are good and selfless men. We have to admit this, even if the dogmas of our own sect tell us that these men are mistaken in their beliefs. But how, if we say that ours, and ours only, is the one true belief, can we admit that men, who live by what we must call false beliefs, are truly saintly in their lives? There is a fallacy somewhere, a contradiction. If we are right, then these men, however saintly, must be wrong. And if, since they are saintly, they are right—then what of us?

Let us allow ourselves to be mistaken. Let us be generous, and cease this warfare, that spoils so much of life's beauty and wastes so much of life's time, over the rights and wrongs of Right and Wrong. Because our neighbour goes to Chapel instead of to Church, he is not necessarily a mistaken person, any more than we are mistaken, as he apparently thinks, because we go to Church instead of Chapel. What applies to us may, surely, apply to him. Besides, we know that we should not judge. And we know how we should treat our neighbour.

But we are trying to find out, in the midst of these contradictions, what it means when we say that a man is religious. Does it mean that he goes regularly to

Church (or Chapel, or the Synagogue, or the Mosque), and must he be irreligious if he does not go regularly to one of these places of worship? There are many deeply and truly religious people who go to church, who go there because they must, because they love God and feel that they can worship Him best in His own house. But perhaps there are others who go to church for other reasons, and who, if they were honest with themselves, would admit these other reasons. And there is no other real reason for going to church than that of wanting with all one's heart to worship God. So it is not necessarily true that all people who go to church are really religious, nor is it necessarily true that all people who do not go to church are really irreligious.

Religion is a personal thing. It concerns our own heart and no one else's, it is between ourselves and God. We have no right to judge others' religion by our own, for, while we have much in common, we are at the same time individuals, and nothing is more individual than our personal religion. The man we think without religion because we never see him in church on Sunday may all the same be a most religious person, for he may worship God, not only on Sunday but every day, in his work, in his family, in the beauty of nature or art, and always in the seclusion of his own heart. The truly religious worship God in secret: how should we know that they worship at all?

They worship God in secret, then, the truly religious, of whatever religion, whatever sect, and to each of them worshipping God is something personal and different. But the evidence of their beliefs, of their recognition of a superhuman power, lies, as the dictionary says, in its effect "on conduct and mental attitude." "By their fruits ye shall know them." But there is sound fruit and unsound fruit, and only that which ripens in the sunlight of true religious conviction is sound. It is possible to appear religious, to make a display of selflessness and virtuousness, and sometimes this display may deceive, but it is not the fruit of true righteousness.

This display of selflessness is really the display of selfishness, set out for our own ends, to gain approval and regard. Its motive is impure, and only the pure motive, that rare flower, leads to the sound fruit. We deceive not only others but ourselves in our motives for doing things. So often we think we do a thing for selfless reasons, and then look a little more closely and find that we have deceived ourselves and that really the reason for our action is a selfish one. It is a depressing discovery. After all, we find, we are mean, competitive persons, bent upon our own ends. And perhaps, more depressing discovery still, the motive that actuated our very desire to be virtuous and selfless was an impure one. We cannot help knowing that the world looks favourably upon those whom it considers "good."

But the desire to be good, which is itself part of religion, is inherent in all of us. Even the sorriest sinner among us comes at times to repent, sees the happiness that would come if he were freed from sin, and longs to be other than what he is. We all long to be something other than what we are, and it is this longing that brings us to religion. There is something in the human spirit that knows good from evil, that craves for release from evil and struggles upwards to the light of goodness. Some men find the way upwards, some die without finding it, and some find it but cannot follow it, and these last are the most unhappy. But we all want to find it. That is why Christ came to save sinners: He knew that they had most need of Him.

Western civilization finds the way upwards in Christianity. Jesus said: "I am the way." He did not say: "I am the only way," but for us He is the finest way, the way of our forefathers, the way of Western tradition, and, although this essay is about religion, which means all kinds of worship and belief in God, it is with Christianity that it must deal. All religions are the same in essence. The sacred books of the East have many passages that coincide with our own Bible, and other teachers used often similar words to those used by Jesus, but there is not space here, nor is it relevant, to discuss comparative religion, though we ought to remember, when we sing such words as "The heathen in his blindness bows down to wood and stone," that the heathen, when he does this, is worshipping God, as we do when we bow our heads in Church.

No one would claim that to follow the way of Christianity is easy. It is the way to the kingdom of heaven, through the strait gate. What is easy is to mistake the path, to make a false journey and arrive nowhere, to travel laden with complicated and unnecessary burdens.

The religious man takes nothing with him but his faith. Faith is difficult to define, and perhaps it cannot be expressed in words: for some spiritual states there are no physical, verbal symbols. But part of faith is that same sense of longing to be other than what one is, the need to move upwards towards a new condition of being. Nothing is more foolish than the saying that you cannot change human nature. Human nature's very essence, its very life, is its capacity for change. Every day of a man's existence sees him changed a little in some way or other: the unchangeable, fundamental constant is the persistent need for change, to move upwards. When a great change takes place in a man, we say that he is converted, like St. Paul or St. Francis.

Psychologists tell us that conversion is only a sudden change as far as our conscious minds go, that really the change has been taking place for a long time in our subconscious minds, and this only bears out the idea of man's perpetual capacity for change. When a man is converted, there comes a flooding in of faith. Not only is he aware that he wants to move forward, to make the perilous journey through the strait gate, but also he knows that, with God's help, he can make the journey and arrive at the Kingdom. But not all those who make the journey need undergo this kind of conversion. The change is as complete in the end if it comes slowly and in gradual perception, and the faith is as strong that is slowly acquired.

We feel ourselves to be weak and helpless, often terribly so, so that all our efforts fail and we see ourselves slipping backwards instead of travelling on. We lose faith then. We believe ourselves alone, unfriended and undirected, and afraid, afraid of ourselves and of other people and of life. But there have been no great men of religion, no saints, who have not felt like this, who have not thought at times that to live rightly and to do what God, or their consciences, wanted them to do was too hard, too bitter. From the greatest to the least they have prayed then that the cup might pass from them. But the next part of that prayer always follows, and nevertheless they follow not their own will but God's, and go on instead of turning back. It is the flesh that is weak, that desires comfort and security, habit and the easier road. The spirit, though, is willing, and the spirit it is that rules us in the end, sending us onward towards the Kingdom. When man raises his arms in prayer, he becomes the sign of the cross. The body is the crucifixion of the spirit, and when we turn to God in prayer we are most tormented, and when we are most tormented we are nearest to peace. When we are most alone, we are nearest to the Prince of Peace, who was a lonely man.

These things, these agonies, come to the religious man. Others, who allow the spirit to be blinded by the flesh, who will not listen to the spirit's urgent demand that they shall begin the journey to the Kingdom, do not feel the torment of loneliness, of loss of faith, do not wander in the wilderness and fall repeatedly back, and stare despair and self-despising in the face. But even so they are not happy, not in the way that the pilgrim is happy, and happy, because he knows despair as an inevitable stage in his journey, even in his despair. They may be rich, they may have high positions, comfort, all the worldly goods they desire, but who has known a really happy rich man, a cabinet minister who had serenity of mind? These things, these riches and satisfactions are illusions. They can be touched and seen, but they are illusions beside the happiness of the saint, that cannot be touched or seen. Those who follow them are "the dead" of whom Jesus spoke, the dead to spiritual aspiration. They too have the love of God, but they will not accept it. It was for them that Christ came, but they will not receive Him. Not one is to blame. You cannot blame the blind or the deaf, and often even the blind come to see, the deaf to hear.

More to blame are those who have eyes but see not, those who hear the calling of the spirit, but will not hear, for they consciously turn away from what they know they ought to do, and to sin consciously has been said to be the sin against the Holy Ghost. But we do not know how many of these are in the midst of a terrible internal conflict, how many are miserable because they are divided against themselves, how many are trying to follow the dictates of the spirit and continually failing. It is for the man who has succeeded to help them.

The great fault lies in those who would become "good" men for their own ends, who would go apart to perfect themselves and forget that others need help. They may do no harm, but to do no good when you have the power to do good is the true failure to be a

Christian. There was no one whom Jesus forgot. When He was dying, He remembered not only to forgive, and so to help, those who had killed Him, but also two thieves whom He had never seen before. It is not those whom he loves that the Christian must especially help, not those near and dear to him, his mother and sister and brothers, but those who are strangers to him, and those who are his enemies.

But we live in a world where these things seem impossible. How are we to live if we do not vie continually with our fellows? Circumstances seem to drive us farther and farther from practical Christianity. We are hardly allowed to be honest. Strictly speaking, few of us do earn our bread honestly, for "business methods" are not based upon honesty but upon shrewdness and competition, on implied trickery and an endless conflict with others. Selfishness is forced upon us. We are the victims of a system that perpetually forces us to behave more like animals than gods. Our human needs have to be satisfied. We must eat, we must mate, we must be entertained, we must work, and, preeminently, we must preserve ourselves. Locked in the vicious circle of modern life, a man may well look out upon the teachings of Jesus and regretfully shrug his shoulders at them, if he does not actually laugh at them: "Give all thou hast," "Love thy neighbour," "Take no thought for the morrow," "Become as little children." These things, in a sophisticated, acquisitive, competitive and conflict-ridden world, seem no more than a bitter joke. The vicious circle holds us fast: we must go on spinning with it or be flung off into oblivion. And daily the pace of the circle's spinning becomes more frantic, the struggle for a living harder, the ant-heap busyness of humanity more and more mechanical and unavoidable.

And beyond our individual lives, what other hope is there? Political parties claim our various allegiance, each promising us what we need, each breaking its promise. Dictators threaten our liberty, if we can still be said to have liberty. Communism offers us civil war, as if everyday life were not civil war enough. Both offer destruction and suffering for some if not for all of us.

Two streets away from our homes, our offices, children play in the gutter because they have nowhere else to play. They are too ill-clad to be protected from the winter wind, they are too ill-nourished to be protected from disease. We do what we can, we provide playgrounds and a little free milk, but still there are children ill-clad, ill-nourished and unable to play anywhere but in the gutter. Their mothers and fathers are no better off. We know this and are sorry and can do nothing. Up and down the country there are hospitals where men and women lie sick and alone and dying. We have provided hospitals, but we have not provided health. There are lunatic-asylums where men who believe themselves Hitler mix with men who believe themselves God, and we outside shake our heads sadly, and forget to wonder whether we ourselves are much saner.

There are other institutions in the depths of the country, where men have lived for the last twenty years and will live until they die. Some of these men have no legs and arms, some of them have no faces: all of them fought in the war of 1914-1918. And we rearm for the next war.

Where are we to see, in the vicious circle, anything but despair? We may turn to this or that in the attempt to forget, to the cinema, to novel-reading, to the making of money, to the dreaming of dreams, but in the end we must return to what actually is, and see it for chaos. We may rail against the system. We may say: "The state of things is terrible, but communism will put it right," or we may put forward any theory or pro- position that takes our fancy. But the system is of our making, the world is what we have made it. To say, now that we have brought it to this pass: "I will now get it right by putting my favourite theory into opera- tion" is nothing more nor less than consummate conceit, for it implies that we are apart from the system, instead of every day contributing to it. There is a beam in our own eye. It might be as well to reform ourselves before we begin to reform the world that our blindness has builded. Reform, like charity, begins, surely, at home.

This applies, too, to our dealings with other countries. We resent the armaments of Germany and France, we resent other countries' claims to a right to exist, but we rearm ourselves as fast as they do, we insist on our right to exist. Are we, then, so superior to all other countries, does England contain better men than Germany, or is it a mistake that we are all equal in the eyes of God? Here again is the vicious circle. If you rearm, we'll rearm. If you manufacture gas-masks at the rate of thousands a day, so will we. If you threaten to attack us, we'll threaten to attack you. If you attack us, we'll attack you one minute sooner. An eye for an eye. Chemists prepare gases, district councils discuss bomb and gas-proof shelters. A chemist at a public meeting informs us that the effects of burning gases can be counteracted by taking a warm bath within twenty minutes of making contact with them, and we feel momentarily comforted, forgetting that it may not be very easy to take a warm bath when a bomb has fallen through the bathroom roof and put the geyser out of commission.

But the chemist means well, and so do the arms manufacturer, the politician, the Fascist, the Communist, the economist, the man in the street. There lies the tragedy. Man is a peace-loving animal, iron though that may seem, and a herd animal that does not deliberately cause his fellows hurt, and he always means well. But he does not mean well enough. We are the victims of the vicious circle. But we have created it, through centuries of blindness and well-meaning, and we are the victims of ourselves.

But is it idealistic and optimistic to think that, beneath the chaos, something begins in these last few years, to stir in men's hearts? Surely that everlasting desire for change still exerts itself. We can say at least that we are not satisfied with the chaotic state of affairs which we have created. In their best aspects, their desires for change and reform, the new political creeds, whether Communist or Fascist, are evidence of this: it is their method that is madness, since they seek to alter the material distress of a materialistic world by materialistic means, to cast out Satan by Satan. You cannot influence material circumstances, as psychology is beginning to show us, except by the mind, the spirit. We think a thing in the abstract of mind, and put it into action in the concrete of matter, and the reverse process is impossible. We must work from within out- wards. While we seek to apply remedies outwardly, leaving the chaos still within, we are doing no more than patching an old garment: a new rent appears, though the patch remains whole, in another part of the worn cloth: we are putting new wine into old wine-skins.

When we come to the consideration of wars and threats of wars and the efforts, so various, so sincere, that are being made to prevent war, the same applies. We may find an effective antidote to poisonous gas but we have only applied a patch, and very soon the danger will break out once more in another direction. The root cause, something within us, the will to war, the will to hate and to fear, is not changed. That may sound as though, for all our efforts against it, we in reality want war. We do not want war, but we are not willing to attain the state of mind, and so the state of conduct, in which war becomes impossible. We are not willing to give up our acquisitiveness, our beliefs in national supremacy, our fear and hatred of other countries, any more than we are willing, really and fundamentally, to give up the hatred and fear that in private life separates us from our brother man. We want peace, honestly and truly enough, but we want it for nothing. The competitive conditions of life dictate that we shall always try to get something for nothing. Peace and love cannot be acquired on those terms. There is such a thing as sacrifice, and if we want a thing we must be prepared to give for it. We must be prepared to give, and to leave the taking to take care of itself. For it will take care of itself, as the bread cast upon the waters returns to us always at last.

Must we say, then, that the efforts we make for peace, our peace-ballots, our anti-war movements, our medical associations for the prevention of war, a hundred other activities directed against the outbreak of another war, are false and meaningless? We know that they are sincere, but is that enough? How easily they become patches applied to the outside of a state of inward and unrealized disruption, how easily we deceive ourselves into believing that to spend our time working on research into the means of preventing war is enough. It is not enough. By their fruits ye shall know them, and, in spite of these many activities, in spite of the well-wishing and hard work of thousands, the threat of war persists.

It is the same with many other kinds of activity for the betterment of the world. We work hard to improve the condition of the poor, housing, nutrition, employment, medical treatment and our hard work satisfies us that we are doing all we can. And much is accomplished. The patched garment can be worn again, until a fresh rent appears. But there are still hungry children, families living in one room, mothers dying in childbirth through lack of nourishment or proper care, young men

standing idle at street-corners because there is no work
for them to do. Can we honestly say that we progress?
We alter things a little, we improve things a little, but
it is like taking water from one part of the ocean and
emptying it into another. The ocean remains as vast,
though its waters are differently disposed. We may give
our time, our labour and our hopes to these good works,
but we will not give our whole hearts, ourselves, a
willing sacrifice. Nothing else but that is enough. If
each of us were willing to starve that the starving might
live then no one would starve: for economists never tire
of telling us that there is sufficient money and sufficient
raw material and sufficient foodstuff in the world, were
it only properly distributed, for us all to live comfortably.

For all our attempts to escape from the vicious circle,
for all our hard work, our well-wishing, our sincerity
and hope, it seems that we remain bound, like Ixion,
to the unceasing wheel. But we want to break free. We
even know a little how to break free. But knowing is a
different state from that of doing and being. The truth,
we know, shall make us free, but it is necessary to be
and to do the truth, to live the truth, before we attain
to freedom. There are signs, though, that many men
and women are growing more and more strongly determined to attempt the breakaway. Even in fiction and
some cinema-films there are the signs of a seeking,
beneath the chaos of material existence, for a faith, a
belief, a truth by which we can live. There is a new
interest in religion, religion often outside the churches,
often so much outside them that they deny its existence

and insist that, on the other hand, the interest in religion is waning. This is only so in the case of the interest in the religion of the established churches. The churches too have become too much part of the materialistic chaos. For centuries they have been aligning themselves not with God but with mammon. The tables of the money-changers are set up once more within the temple. Realizing this, those who truly seek religion, seek it elsewhere. It is for the churches, like individuals, to look for the beam in their own eye before they condemn the people for staying away from their services.

There is a stirring, like the stirring of the earth that moves forward towards the spring while winter's snow yet binds its surface, in our inward hearts. Many people feel that soon there must come a parting of the ways, and perhaps this is so. We know that all previous civilizations have reached a pitch of material inventiveness, culture and sophistication, and have then, often through the agency of a great war, crashed like an undermined building, or slowly declined to insignificance. It is not difficult to draw parallels between this moment of our own civilization and those last heights of apparent wisdom, success and power that have preceded the disintegration of earlier civilizations.

But there is no reason why our civilization must inevitably crash in ruins. Because a thing has happened many times in the past, because the vicious circle in the past has always attained so terrific a pace that, like a faulty fly-wheel, it has finally flown in pieces, that is no reason why it should happen again in

the future. But it will happen, unless we can break
free from the vicious circle, unless, when we come to
the parting of the ways, we can take that which lies at
a tangent to it. And it is with the object of being able
when the time comes to avert the catastrophe and
choose the right path that we are bestirring ourselves,
beneath the surface, to seek a new life, a new ethic.
But there is no time to lose, for we know not when
the parting of the ways cometh. Those who do not
watch will miss it, and it will be gone like a wraith in
the night.

We know what is the matter with present-day
existence, we know that it has given materialism first
place and the things of the spirit second, we know that
we try to worship both God and Mammon, and,
finding this impossible, worship Mammon, we know
that we are trying to put new wine in old wine-skins,
and that our sincerity, our kindness, our bravery and
our pity, real though they are, still are not enough to
alter the world and make order of chaos, light of darkness. The modern world, like the individuals who live
in it, is sick. The matter with it is an insidious illness
which we may call enslavement to the vicious circle.
But there must, further, be a prime cause of that sickness, and we shall not have approached the root of the
matter until we know what that cause is. At the same
time, while the world is sick in its material aspects, it
is not dying. The life of a world, like that of a man, is
its spiritual life, and the spirit is immortal. A world, a
civilization, may crumble, like a human body, to dust,
but something remains, the spirit, life itself, the breath

that animates. This is a matter of faith, that cannot be proven and needs no proof, since it is known in our inmost hearts. But the spirit can be, as it were, anæsthetized, so that the man it animates becomes one of "the dead," unmindful of the spiritual aspect of life. And if a man be one of the dead, he will miss the parting of the ways and continue to wander in the wilderness. But it is possible for one of these dead to awaken in the spirit, like a patient coming round from an anæsthetic, to become, slowly or suddenly, converted and aware of a new light shed upon his every-day life. It is possible for him to become a "religious man," whose conduct and mental attitude depend upon the recognition of "a superhuman power." A man who is in this way a religious man, who does not merely think about God and pray to God, but knows God for part of himself and allows his religion to bear fruit in his actions and his behaviour towards his fellows has already taken the first steps along the tangential path that leads out of the vicious circle. He is already a pilgrim on the way to the Kingdom of Heaven; but the Kingdom of Heaven is not a place that we can "go" to; it is within us, a thing that we can become part of.

Yet something prevents the human being from starting upon this pilgrimage, from doing more than thinking about it. Even if a man is not still one of "the dead," even if he is coming slowly to realize that there is only one hope for him, bound as he is by the materialistic bonds of life's competition and strife and greed, if he wants to be whole and free and sane, yet still something prevents us.

There are not many of us who do not, at least at
fleeting moments of our lives, want to make the pilgrimage. But there are not many of us who make it,
and, if we knew why this was, we should be at the root
of the matter. Why, knowing that the ethics of our
daily lives are hateful, aware that, for all our efforts,
we do not progress, are we unable to change our
human nature and follow another ethic, one which we
know but do not live, and why are we unable to
progress towards a new world?

The "new" ethic, the religion, for Western man, is
that founded upon the teaching of Jesus: not the dogma
of the churches, which has perverted much of the
teaching of Jesus, but the teaching itself, as we find it in
the Gospels. Few people will deny, though many will
dismiss it as impossible of achievement, that to carry
out in one's daily life the commandments Jesus gave
us would mean that we should become different men
and women, that "human nature had been changed"
in us. But what, faced with the necessity to embrace
Christianity in its present implications, must the would-
be pilgrim inevitably feel? He must feel afraid, and
the root of the matter, the root-cause of the strife and
competition and hatred and selfishness of life is fear.

It is not simply that fear prevents us from becoming
Christians in the full sense of the word, prevents us
because to be Christians seems to ask that we make
ourselves vulnerable by the material world and by
those who adhere to it. On the other hand, fear drives
us deeper into the material world. There is no middle
course, no way of living between two worlds, in a

region where we can escape both and the fears that both impose upon us. If anything is true of life, it is that it has to be lived to the full. Whether materially or spiritually, you must grasp life and live it with all your power, or it will elude you and leave you behind. To turn away from life, whichever of these two kinds of life you have chosen, means to be left stranded, your hands and your heart left full of nothing but a negative emptiness. It is perhaps better to live even the wickedest life to the full: at least then one does not do violence to life itself, one is not negative. The man who is never very wicked and never very good creates nothing and continuously cancels himself out. The only brave thing to do is to go the whole hog. God forgives the great sinner as readily as the petty sinner: and the greater the sin the sweeter the forgiveness, the more enduring the conversion, when the power that has been used, as it was by many saints in their earlier years, for great sin can be used for as great goodness.

Fear prevents us from being great sinners, just as it prevents us from being great saints. To escape it, we try to live between these two worlds of materialism and spirituality, to make a continual compromise. The terrible truth seems to be that the circumstances of modern life, while they demand that, to earn one's daily bread, one should be a petty sinner, deny the good man a place. The compromise is forced upon us. While, to keep our foothold, we have to be dishonest, to be ruthless, to compete, to scramble over the back of the man in front regardless of how he will fare, we endeavour to strike a balance by our daily kindness and sympathy, the copper we give to a street-singer, the down-and-out we befriend. But in this way we make no progress: the two cancel one another, and leave us still where we were, struggling for livelihood, our hearts aching for the misfortunes of our fellows. And above all, our consciences are never quite at rest.

Fear of losing the race, of being beaten by the man behind, of being outdone by our neighbour, of losing social or financial position, of disgrace, of being misunderstood and made to feel outcast, all these things keep us imprisoned in the great competition, the endless strife, greed and selfishness of personal and of national and international life. Fear forces social insincerity upon us, makes us turn away from others' troubles. We have enough troubles of our own. We shall lose pace in the race if we turn aside to help the man who has fallen. We shall be classed with him and have to take on his burden.

We fear the future because we do not know what will happen next. We fear the past because it has an unfortunate aptitude for returning to us and reproaching us. We fear our fellow-men because we do not know how friendly or unfriendly they are to us, or what they will do to us next. So we do not dare to behave sincerely to them, to give ourselves in friendship and co-operation, unless we envisage from that friendship or co-operation some advantage to ourselves. And we fear ourselves, because we do not know ourselves, and cannot tell what ridiculous or dangerous step our unknown and uncertain selves may not lead us to take to-morrow or next week. So we come to fear life, and to want to escape it, and to make compromises with it. We bargain with it, as we do with our fellows: If you'll behave decently to me, I'll behave decently to you. If you don't, I won't. This is the perpetual conversation, that comes over frontiers and dividing seas, between nation and nation. Fear, between men or between countries, comes always in the end to strife, the final desperate effort not to be outdone, to preserve our lives, and our possessions and our territories.

It is this fear that rises like a barrier between the individual and the acceptance of the religious, the Christian life. It bars the way out of the vicious circle, the beginning of the pilgrim's path. Christianity demands sacrifice, giving without counting the cost or taking thought for the morrow or for personal advantage. How are we to behave like this, if the man next door is going to continue in the old way? How shall we live ourselves if we are always giving and making no provision for ourselves, how fail to be left behind in the race, ignored, starved, ridiculed, outcast? Fear simply will not allow us to contemplate such circumstances. We are herd-animals and we do not know how to live outside the herd. We feel that we should be helpless were we deliberately to divorce ourselves from the herd, as this true practice of Christianity would demand. For it does demand divorce from the herd's activities, which is different from divorce from our fellow men, in that a man cannot be a Christian and keep on with these manifestations of herd-life that our fear imposes on us, dishonesty, compromise, competition, self-regard. Herd-life it-self is the outcome of the fear to stand alone.

Yet the practice of Christianity does not demand that we be born supermen, as might at first seem to be the case. There is not one among us who is not po-tentially the kind of superman who can stand alone and, not merely continue to exist in a herd-world mad with materialistic activities, but live more fully than we ever dreamed it possible to live. For man does not live by bread, or material possessions in the shape of money, goods, or position, alone. Each one of us is made in the image of God. Each one of us can live by every word that proceedeth out of the mouth of God, for potentially man is God, and the Kingdom of God is within him. Only when we make the word of God, who is ourselves, real to us, only when we learn to know ourselves for what we really are and to live in the Kingdom of God, which is the same as being com-pletely in possession of ourselves, do we begin truly to live.

In the herd, the vicious circle, we know almost nothing of ourselves. We are cogs in a wheel, useful to keep the wheel turning (if there lies any virtue in doing so), but helpless as individuals. The wheel makes so much clatter as it turns, deafening us as it takes us with it, that we cannot hear the word that proceedeth out of the mouth of God, by which we should live.

Again it is necessary to escape the wheel of life. But escape may be a misleading word, since it implies running away. We cannot escape things by running

away, for they pursue: or, since generally we are really
running away from ourselves, we take them with us.
The only escape lies in going straight on, and coming
out at last on the other side. It is useless to strive
against our imprisonment in the circle. The circle
is of our own making: only ourselves can make our
way out of it. And strife has never been a profitable
means of attaining anything, for, even if we seem to
attain something as a result of strife, sooner or later
strife breaks out again, the attainment is not permanent.
For that reason there will never be a war to end war.
Strife breeds strife, within international relations, or
within our individual selves. It is an attempt to cast
out evil by evil, to cast out Satan by Satan. To escape,
we must not strive, but accept. We must accept the
vicious circle, accept our imprisonment in it, and stop
resenting and hating it and trying to overcome its
evil by more evil, the evil of hatred and warfare. And,
having accepted, we must go through it and emerge
into the daylight on the other side.

It is the hardest thing in the world, or seems to be to
us who are so used to strife and fear, to love evil and
to love our enemies, to overcome evil by good, but it
is what the man who would be a Christian must do.
Acceptance is only another word for love, which is
another word for truth, and only the truth shall make
us free. By accepting the vicious circle, by accepting
all the unsatisfactory and uncomfortable circumstances
of life, we begin already to put ourselves a little outside
the circle. When we are striving against them, at grips
with them, we are too close to them, too deeply

immersed, to see them. Acceptance, or love, stands a little apart and looks on what it loves.

The business of dealing with the system, with social distress and unrest and unsatisfactoriness, begins, then, with dealing with the distress, the conflict in oneself. "Be still, and know that I am God." We must learn to know ourselves, and so to know God, and, knowing ourselves for what we are, to escape selfishness. We must accept ourselves, and, in accepting, cease fearing ourselves and warring with ourselves. We must love ourselves, not with subjective selfishness such as the phrase usually implies, but objectively, looking upon ourselves as we can sometimes look on others whom we love, as a queer and disconcerting mixture of good and bad, known and unknown, often pretty abominable, sometimes rather nice, but always to be forgiven and never, whatever they do, to forfeit our love. If we can achieve this, we have once more got a little way outside, this time outside the microcosmic vicious circle of ourselves, which is a part and a reflection of the macrocosmic one, which is the social system made by us.

We know that the Christian may not judge. He may reason and feel and compare and deliberate, but he may not condemn. He may not even condemn himself, for that only produces more conflict in himself. And he may not condemn his fellows. He may not be righteous. Other people do some pretty terrible things, but, don't we, too? We have no right, it simply is not fair, to condemn others. On paper it looks so simple: in practice it is so difficult, because fear, again,

leads us to condemnation: we feel more worthy ourselves if we can point out another's unworthiness. In
four words, however there is only one thing that the
Christian must do about his opinions of others: mind
his own business.

If we could give up a little our habit of condemning
the evil we see in others we should soon discover how
much good there is in them that we were blinded to
while we were making much ado about their faults.
And the more good we saw in them, the more we should
love them. Obedience to one Christian commandment
brings obedience to another with it. If we do not
judge our neighbour, we shall find ourself, conversely,
loving him.

But to be honest with ourselves comes first. It is
easy to think we love humanity, easy to go about with
that loving smile that is nothing but a mask and deceives
no one but its wearer. And to be honest with ourselves,
we must, once more, love ourselves: and that does not
mean be indulgent toward ourselves, though it
does mean be forgiving toward ourselves. If we can
make peace with ourselves, making peace with others
will be comparatively easy.

Faith is a very little understood word. It is thought
that some people have faith, while others do not. But
we all have faith in something, the financier in money,
the artist in art, the priest in his religion. What is
difficult to realize is that God is not a being separate
from everyday life, but the breath of everyday life.
God is in money, in art and in religion, and in every
other manifestation of life. All men have faith in some

aspect of God. Because great wealth can be mis-used, it is not true to say that money is evil. It can be very well-used. It can help suffering, and at once becomes God-like in its compassion and strength. It is the misuse of the thing we have faith in, the misuse of our God, that it is necessary to change. But, just as we are made in God's image and too are inspired with His breath, so we make God in our own image, and not until we have made something useful of ourselves, until we have learnt the right use of ourselves, shall we properly imagine and make use of whatever God, money, art, religion or whatever you choose, we worship. Faith in God must eventually come to mean faith in ourselves, who are potentially God.

But fear, just as it tears us apart in conflicts and makes us useless to ourselves or to anyone else, can destroy faith. A man might feel a sudden faith in Christianity, and determine to lead a Christian life. But fear of what he thought leading a Christian life implied in the way of standing alone, of sacrifice and love for others, might destroy his faith. But, similarly, his faith might destroy his fear.

Jesus said: "He that believeth on me shall have the light of life." There is no one, nothing, else for the religious man, the man who would be a Christian, to turn to in his uncertainties, his conflicts and despairs. "Come unto me, and I will give you rest." It is impossible for conflict to exist where Jesus is. It is impossible not to be at peace if one is in the presence of Jesus, and that presence is never withheld from any one who seeks it. We know the things that Jesus said and did: we need no other guide when we are trying to emancipate ourselves from the chaos in which we find ourselves and the world from the chaos in which we know it to be.

It has been said before, often enough, that Christianity, if we could all practise it, would save this civilization from the ruin towards which it seems to so many people to be rushing. Nothing could be more true, and nothing less useful than to go on saying it. To say it is not enough: we must be and do. There will come, before many years are over, a point at which we may take one road or other, a cross-roads almost certainly labelled *War* and *Peace*. Enough prophets have told us what war would mean, unthinkable suffering and horror, plague, the extermination of a vast portion of civilized humanity, the end of the civilization the centuries have built up. Many, too, think this wholesale destruction inevitable, even "right," a part of universal law, as it has seemed to be in the past. But this building up and destroying of civilizations is part of the law of the vicious circle, and we can break the law by breaking the circle before the destruction-point is reached. We can take the road labelled *Peace* when we come to the parting of the ways. And we are striving already, as has been said, to do this, our faint inward stirrings towards some kind of religion, some kind of change in human nature, are indications that we are, beneath the chaotic surface, casting about for some kind of salvation. It is two thousand years since Jesus came to save sinners, but it is difficult to think of any better way of salvation that has been invented, even in all that time. Besides, He said, I am the way, and that surely, is enough for us.

Movements made to abolish war should not, as they so often are, be called anti-war movements. That name implies war against war, the strife to cast out Satan by Satan. Again, we must accept. We must accept a man when he takes up a belligerent attitude toward us, and love him in spite of it. For he is not always belligerent: in five minutes time he will be lending a friend a pound-note, or carrying home a tired child. We could love him doing those things. We can love him when he wants to hurt us, for those other actions of his are still just as real. Nor do we do any good if we hit back when he attacks us, or even get in our blow first. It only makes him more angry. We can refuse to fight with him, however. But the immediate supposition is that he will knock us down. Very well, why not? At least we shall not have contributed to the fight and put ourselves as much "in the wrong" as we think him. But there is much more to turning the other cheek than that. Try it next time (if there is such a time) a man wants to hit you. He won't hit you, and there will be an end of it. Could you hit a man whom you knew to be virtually defenceless? We're often base, but seldom as base as that. That the man has not hit you may seem inexplicable, but it becomes less so if you put yourself in his position. How would you feel if you had threatened someone who had looked at you squarely and answered that he would not fight you? You would feel humiliated. You would feel that his spiritual courage was greater than your physical courage, and that you had made an ass of yourself. But you would not quite know why. You would only know that you were up against something you could not understand. You were up against forgiveness and love. For one must not use what is called passive resistance for one's own ends, to get one out of a nasty licking. One must use it for the sake of the man who threatened you, because you don't want him to let himself down, because you don't want him to be hurt, because you are sorry for his anger and understand it, and know that he is a human being like yourself, and to be loved instead of striven against.

But suppose he wants to fight you, as often happened when one was a schoolboy and still, in effect, happens now one is grown up, because you have something that he wants or because he thinks you have done him some injury. He may be right. The sensible and civilized thing to do is to give it to him. He wants it, and that is reason enough. Besides, it may make him happy to have it, and to make him happy will not make you unhappy: on the contrary. Nothing that we possess is comparable in value to the happiness we should have in being without it because we had given it to someone else. Man cannot live by bread alone.

All this applies, of course, to countries that go to war or want to go to war. There is only one way to cast out fear, which is hatred, which is war. Perfect love casteth out fear, and hatred and war. If we could learn to love, then war would be impossible, defences, bomb-proof shelters, anti-aircraft guns, armaments, treaties a ridiculous mockery, the paraphernalia of the fear we had outgrown. Suppose a nation were to see in time the cross-roads approaching, suppose it were to wrest itself away from the habit of centuries, the age-old fears, the habit of hatred, and to choose, because it had listened to its own conscience, the road marked *Peace*. And suppose it said to the world at large: We will never again join war with any other country. We renounce the madness, the shame and the sin of killing. We will make no more guns, and we will melt down those we have, using the metal of them for more civilized and humane purposes, the money we have hitherto spent on them to make the lives of our people easier. We have burnt the formulas for poison gas. We have demobilized our army and navy and air force. We offer you peace, or if you will not accept peace, our lives to the glory of Peace.

And suppose that country were England.

There are men, perhaps, who could still find it in their hearts to take advantage of that demobilized, dis-armed and defenceless country. There were men who crucified Jesus. It is possible that dictators, men so insane with the desire for power that they cannot be treated as ordinary beings, would order their armies to attack. But those armies would have to be reckoned with. They would be composed of men like the inhabitants of the country against whom they were sent out. They might be filled with the mass-hysteria that moves an army as one man. But would they be able, even so, to gas, to bomb, to shoot, to crush and conquer the men and women and children who had done them no harm and whom, before their dictator told them otherwise, they recognized for their brothers and sisters? It is impossible to believe. They would return to their dictators, and their dictators would be powerless.

England can be that disarmed, disarming country. The spirit of Christianity in England, together with our native tolerance and our native humanity and common sense, can make it so. Just as mass-feeling contributes towards the brutality of war, so it can contribute to the loving-kindness of peace. We have had the courage to make war, and to die in battle. We have the courage to make peace, and if necessary to die in sacrifice. We have an example. What is the loss of our own life, even if we achieved nothing for the peace of the world but the preservation of the lives of our enemies, if we die because we believe in Christ? For, believing on Him, we should exchange life for eternal life.

It is with this decision that we shall sooner or later be faced, the decision between the roads marked *War* and *Peace*. Nor can we believe that we should ever be called upon to sacrifice our lives and those of those dear to us. To turn the other cheek disarms one's opponent. To be determined for peace creates peace. If one country will come to this determination, and it does not matter in the least whether it be England or any other, these others will follow suit. We are sick of the thought and the threat of war. No nation, as a congregation of individuals, wants war. But nations are afraid, and cannot overcome their fear. Let one lay down its arms, overcome its fear, look death and destruction in the face for the sake of humanity and for the sake of Jesus who died for humanity, and the others will find their fear vanished and lay down their arms with relief.

The decision for peace, however, would be only a part, only one of the outcomes of the earlier decision for Christianity. And the same sequence of events follows the decision of one man, ten men, a hundred men, for Christianity. We are afraid to become Christians, as countries are afraid to disarm, because we feel that by doing so we should make ourselves defenceless. We forget that there is no stronger defence than love, the whole armour of God. We forget that there is no happiness greater than self-sacrifice. We forget that if we have love, or God who is love, with us we may walk through the valley of the shadow and fear nothing, suffer no hurt. Let one man here, one man there, remember these things, and lay down his competition, his greed, his self-regard. Others will see him and follow suit. They will marvel at his happiness. They will be incredulous that a man can be happy and satisfied in the possession of nothing but a pure heart and the sight of God, but they will see that it is so, and break away from the circle that binds them and begin the pilgrimage towards a new world.

It looks so difficult. And yet it is so easy. It is easy because it is what, in our hearts, we want to do. How tired we are of the struggle of condemnation and hatred, the inward conflict with our consciences. How miserably we hear Jesus say, Come unto me, and do not come because we are afraid for our money, our selfishness, our fellows' approval. The chaos and complication of life prevents us. We dare not let go, but we long to be free. We make excuses, like the man who wanted to go and bury his father. We cannot bring ourselves to sacrifice our possessions, and go unhappily away like the rich young man. But these excuses are not valid. Nothing is valid but the desire in our hearts for a new life, nothing is valid but the words, Come unto me.

Shall we not become as little children and find again children's happiness? Shall we not give up condemnation and know the freedom of being no longer condemned? Shall we not consider the lilies, be simple, free from vanity and the haunting fear of the morrow? Shall we not look within ourselves and set our house in order for the coming of the Lord, who will make that house the kingdom of heaven which is within us? We can at least make a start. Some of us may fall by the way, but there will be others to help us up. Some of us will feel that we have failed, and give up the journey, and then hear again the words, Come unto me, and go on once more. The way is strait and narrow. There are gardens of Gethsemane to be passed through. There may be a cross on a hill-top at the end of the road, but beyond the cross is eternal life.

We are so near already. We cannot bear to see the suffering of the poor and disinherited. We pity the sick and the maimed. We long for freedom in ourselves and the power through it to help others. Yet we are bound by circumstance and fear. We cannot bring ourselves not to take thought for the morrow, to become as little children and make simple the bewildering complication of our daily lives. We say we do not know how to change. We say it is too difficult, even if we know how.

We pretend to ourselves that everything is really all right. Or we say it will come right, presently. Or we say it's no affair of ours. Or we rail against the system and refuse to see the beam in our own eyes.

But we do know how to change. We know the difference between love and hatred, strife and peace, light and darkness. And we know how to become sane men, whole men who are God, who have the Kingdom of God within them. For we know, and need to know nothing more, that Jesus said before He died: "One last commandment I give unto you: my little children, love one another."